Her Way: The Remarkable Story of Hephzibah Jenkins Townsend

The names of Annie Armstrong and Lottie Moon are forever linked to the missionary movement among Baptists. But behind these well-known leaders lies a vast array of women who cultivated and nurtured the soil for missions years before. Hephzibah Jenkins Townsend was one of those entrepreneurial spirits who forged a path for missions when women were not accepted as leaders. In her story we see the true meaning of sacrificial giving and the power of one voice to change our culture and world. May her example inspire us to rise to the challenge in our day.

> — Wanda Lee, Executive Director
> Woman's Missionary Union, Southern Baptist Convention

As a result of Hephzibah Jenkins Townsend's unwavering commitment to Christ, she blazed the missions trail for all of us. Her sheer determination and "where there's a will, there's a way" attitude is a reminder that each of us can make a difference in the lives of others. The wonderful research and the intriguing way Rosalie Hunt shares Hephzibah's story will encourage you in your service. May we all be found as faithful as Hephzibah.

> — Linda Cooper, President
> Woman's Missionary Union, Southern Baptist Convention

Rosalie Hunt takes us back in time to the low country of South Carolina — with its pluff-mud scents and tabby-oven aromas — through the dramatic life story of Hephzibah Jenkins Townsend, foremother of women's mission organizations. As the story unfolds of a woman living within the societal constraints of the nineteenth century but with an unprecedented zeal for world missions, you will be encouraged — no, you will be compelled — to become like Hephzibah, a woman who lives boldly for Christ through a missions lifestyle and who leaves a missions legacy for succeeding generations.

> — Debby Akerman, Past President
> Woman's Missionary Union, Southern Baptist Convention

As Rosalie Hunt so eloquently states, "It all began with a small group of women meeting at Bleak Hall in 1811." Before there was a Lottie or Annie, there was a Hephzibah, and her missions legacy is undeniable. If you thought, as did I, that Southern Baptists missions began in 1888, you will want to read this book.

— David George, President
Woman's Missionary Union Foundation

History celebrates the famous 1806 Haystack Revival in Williams, Massachusetts, as the beginning of the foreign mission movement in the United States. Few are aware that about the same time, in South Carolina, a young woman's missionary zeal had been kindled by the preaching of Richard Furman, a leading Baptist voice of that time. A year before the New England group sent out its first missionaries in 1812, Hephzibah Jenkins Townsend crystallized her missionary passion by forming the South's first missionary society for women at Bleak Hall, her home on Edisto Island in Charleston County.

In 1813, the work of the two mission movements crossed when Hephzibah met Luther Rice, one of the first missionaries appointed from the Haystack Revival group. From that time on, Hephzibah's missionary society model became the blueprint for supporting missions for countless groups across the United States. In 1888, more than 40 years after her death, the Woman's Missionary Union was officially organized at the national level. Today, WMU is synonymous with missions, and both owe much to the work of a mostly unknown lady from South Carolina. It is time Baptists knew her story.

— Bob Terry, Editor
The Alabama Baptist

Every era of our missions history is challenged by the needs of a hurting world, and every era of our missions involvement is fueled by the missionary zeal of people like Hephzibah Jenkins Townsend. A young woman ahead of her time, Hepzhibah was spirited, courageous, creative — and maybe even a little manipulative. There is no way to overestimate the importance of Hephzibah to the history of Baptist women in missions, and there is no way to really understand Hephzibah's story without the master storyteller Rosalie Hunt.

— Ruby Fulbright, Vice President
North American Baptist Women's Union

Her Way

THE REMARKABLE STORY OF
HEPHZIBAH JENKINS TOWNSEND

ROSALIE HALL HUNT

Her Way: The Remarkable Story of Hephzibah Jenkins Townsend

ISBN: 978-1-940645-31-5

Cover: Bleak Hall, circa 1800, built by Daniel and Hephzibah Townsend. This oil painting is in the possession of a descendant of Hephzibah Jenkins Townsend.

 COURIER PUBLISHING

Greenville, South Carolina

PUBLISHED IN THE UNITED STATES OF AMERICA

DEDICATION

To our beloved physician, Dr. Albert Lee Smith III:
He scattered bright beams wherever he went.

Rosalie Hall Hunt

Lora Danley 4/2018

Foreword

I suppose I first "met" Hephzibah Jenkins Townsend when I moved to South Carolina more than twenty years ago. However, it wasn't until I was doing research for a state missions video that I really "got to know" her. I visited her home and her burial site. I read about her in our history books. I became fascinated by this strong, courageous woman — a woman on whose shoulders I have the privilege of standing.

Several years ago, I had the joy of introducing Hephzibah to Rosalie Hunt. Not surprisingly, she, too, felt an immediate bond with Hephzibah and right away began to talk about telling her story.

I was able to take part in one of Rosalie's research trips. What a delight it was to see her at work, digging out the smallest details of this amazing woman's life — details that will be meaningful to many who read her story.

Hephzibah Jenkins Townsend was a woman who stood on her convictions, even in the face of difficulty and adversity. She was resourceful, loyal, compassionate, and exhibited a servant's heart — qualities that would serve each of us well today, two hundred years later.

I am thankful that you now have the opportunity to meet and be inspired by my "friend" Hephzibah through the words of my friend Rosalie.

Laurie Register
Executive Director-Treasurer
South Carolina Woman's Missionary Union

PREFACE

Her story is better than fiction, for the amazing experiences in her life and the legacy she left are printed in indelible ink. Oddly enough, however, her life story has never been told. The missionary society she founded in 1811 was the forerunner of hundreds of societies that followed and in 1888 became Woman's Missionary Union. Adventure, tragedy, intrigue, triumph, love and perseverance have teamed up in the remarkable life of Hephzibah Jenkins Townsend.

Her life began with danger. Charleston, South Carolina, was a city under siege by the British when Hephzibah was born there in 1780. She was only five days old when her mother died, causing two old servants to risk their own lives to save baby Hephzibah. Ever after, Hephzibah considered slaves as "her people" and this profoundly influenced the direction of her life.

Born at the forging of a new nation, Hephzibah both influenced her times and in turn was impacted by them. She was a trailblazer, a person whose force of character was never in doubt. Beautiful, headstrong, a person of deep integrity, she never went unnoticed. No typical Southern belle, she — a fact to which her husband could ruefully attest. A distant relative, Daniel Townsend was twenty-one years her senior but loved her unreservedly and she returned his devotion in full measure. Theirs was a lifelong love story.

Hephzibah caught the fire of missions zeal from her pastor, the eminent Dr. Richard Furman, and she determined to organize women to support the cause of Christ in other lands. In the

America of 1800, all of a woman's property was controlled by her husband. When Daniel was unwilling to release funds from her inheritance to support missions giving, Hephzibah started a baking venture, and her dear friend and servant Bella became her business partner. They baked cakes and started an enterprise that ended up as a catering business, making Hephzibah Townsend the first female entrepreneur on Edisto Island.

Then in late 1813 when Hephzibah met Dr. Luther Rice, sharing the gospel became an even greater passion for her. Through her baking business, the mission society offerings flourished and Hephzibah Townsend was able to fulfill her dream of building a Baptist church on Edisto. Nearly all its membership was made up of enslaved people and Hephzibah rejoiced to see the spiritual growth in their lives. Although tragedy hit her family time and again and though she lost more than half of her children to deadly diseases, her faith and courage never wavered.

In the latter years of her life, a remarkable revival broke out among the slaves of Edisto. Hephzibah had the joy of assisting her pastor in baptizing sixty new believers the day after Christmas. For a woman to do such a thing would be a singular event in any period of time, but especially so in nineteenth-century America. Force of character and a profound sense of justice were the hallmarks of Hephzibah Jenkins Townsend's life, making her a sterling example of faith and fortitude.

This extraordinary person was a pioneer in missions, a testimony to both unwavering commitment and sheer determination. The footprints of Hephzibah Jenkins Townsend are cemented in the missions history of an entire denomination.

All people of faith in our millennium can look to her and give thanks for such courage that paved the way for this generation and continues to impact our sense of God's call. We follow in her footprints.

Cast of Characters

Bekins, Evelyn — Governess/tutor for the children of Captain Daniel Jenkins

Bella — Servant in the Jenkins home who became a beloved friend and helper to Hephzibah Jenkins Townsend

Furman, Richard (1755-1825) — Pastor, First Baptist Church, Charleston, South Carolina, and pastor to Hephzibah Townsend

Furman, Rachel — Oldest daughter of Richard Furman and friend of Hephzibah Townsend

Jane — Servant in the Jenkins home and head cook

Jack — Servant and husband of Maum Jean, who saved Hephzibah Jenkins's life as a baby

Jenkins, Captain Daniel (1751-1801) — Revolutionary soldier and father of Hephzibah Jenkins

Jenkins, Daniel Junior (1778-1804) — Brother of Hephzibah Jenkins

Jenkins, Hephzibah Frampton (1761-1780) — Mother of Hephzibah Jenkins who died in childbirth

Jenkins, Martha Seabrook (1758-1802) — Second wife of Captain Daniel Jenkins

Jenkins, Mary Caroline (1813-1889) — Wife of John Ferrars Townsend

Jenkins, Richard (1729-1772) — Planter and father of Captain Daniel Jenkins

Joseph — Carpenter at Bleak Hall and husband of Bella

LaRoche, Martha Jenkins (1792-1859) — Half sister of Hephzibah Townsend

Lewis — Son of Bella and Joseph and a skilled carpenter

Ludlow, Rev. Peter — For a short time, pastor of Edisto Baptist Church

Manly, Rev. Basil (1798-1868) — Pastor of First Baptist Church, Charleston, following the death of Richard Furman

Maum Jean — Elderly servant who saved Hephzibah's life as an infant

Maum Nancy — Nursemaid to the Townsend children

McDunn, Rev. William — Later pastor of Edisto Baptist Church and a friend to Hephzibah Townsend

Mikell, Amarinthia Townsend (1810-1852) — Third daughter of Hephzibah and Daniel Townsend

Mikell, Isaac Jenkins — Husband of Amarinthia Townsend

Murray, Abigail Jenkins (1749-1809) — Double cousin of Captain Daniel Jenkins and "Aunt Abby" to young Hephzibah Jenkins

Pinckney, Eliza — Daughter of Charles Cotesworth Pinckney and friend of Hephzibah

Pope, John Theus — Husband of Mary Frampton Townsend

Pope, Mary Frampton Townsend (1804-1861) — Oldest daughter of Hephzibah and Daniel Townsend

Smith, Thomas Peter (1814-1903) — Husband of Theodora Elizabeth Townsend

Smith, Theodora Elizabeth Townsend (1820-1899) — Youngest daughter of Hephzibah and Daniel Townsend

Townsend, Benjamin Joseph (1815-1834) — Son of Hephzibah and Daniel Townsend

Townsend, Daniel II (1720-1784) — Father of Daniel III and great-grand-father of Hephzibah Jenkins Townsend

Townsend, Daniel III (1759-1842) — Husband of Hephzibah Jenkins

Townsend, Daniel Jenkins (1811-1885) — Son of Hephzibah and Daniel Townsend, medical doctor and owner of Fenwick Hall

Townsend, Hephzibah Jenkins (1780-1847) — Daughter of Captain Daniel Jenkins, founder of the first mite society in the South and founder of Edisto Baptist Church

Townsend, John Ferrars (1799-1881) — Oldest surviving son of Hephzibah and Daniel Townsend; planter and state senator

Townsend, Susan Martha (1805-1872) — Second daughter of Hephzibah and Daniel Townsend

Wilkerson, William — Husband of Amarinthia Jenkins

Wilkerson, Amarinthia Jenkins (1790-1878) — Beloved half sister of Hephzibah Jenkins Townsend

TABLE OF CONTENTS

ILLUSTRATIONS

Cover: Bleak Hall

THE REMARKABLE STORY OF
HEPHZIBAH JENKINS TOWNSEND

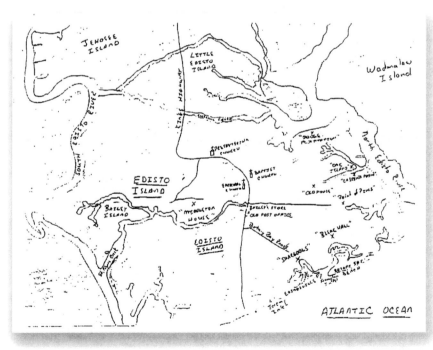

Hand-sketched map of Bleak Hall and surroundings, as it appeared in 1820. (Courtesy of Sherri L. McIntosh (Thesis) University of West Virginia, Morgantown, Virginia, 1998.)

~ One ~

MAY 1780

THE SIEGE

The silence of the May night was nearly touchable. Crickets chirped as usual and an occasional owl called from a nearby tree, but the damp stillness was almost frightening, as if the city walked on tiptoe. Charleston was under siege with British troops encamped on all sides and the firing of cannons sporadically penetrating the eerie silence. It was the year of our Lord 1780, and the beleaguered city seemed to await its fate with resignation.

A light puffy fog groped its way down the quiet length of Calhoun Street. At the three-story house about halfway down the block not a light could be seen. This home of the Jenkinses' of Edisto Island stood empty much of the year; occasionally Captain Jenkins and his young wife, Hephzibah, would come to town and then the house would pulse with life. It appeared unoccupied at the moment, with no one close by to inhale the fragrance of the Carolina jessamine whose heady scent perfumed the stillness of the May evening. The fragrance mingled with the scent of the tea olive and banana shrubs clustered around the deserted front porch.

But appearances can deceive. There might be no visible sign of life, but in the basement there on Calhoun Street the flickering light of a kerosene lantern made out the forms of a young woman lying on a chaise lounge, and the stooped figures of two elderly servants, hovering anxiously near the recumbent form. Hephzibah Jenkins was clutching the hands of Maum Jean. There had never been a time when Hephzibah had *not* had Maum Jean in her life. Jean and her husband, Jack, were house servants of Hephzibah's mother and father before Hephzibah even entered this world. The Framptons, in fact, owned Maum Jean and Jack and their parents before them. Hephzibah loved the old couple who were family to her. Her own mother, Theodora, died when she was young, so Maum Jean was a central figure in the life of the young woman.

Just weeks earlier, Hephzibah, her hopes so high, traveled with Maum Jean and Jack to Charleston to be with Daniel. Stationed in Charleston, her dashing young husband was a captain in the Revolutionary Army and Hephzibah was exceedingly proud of him. She left their little toddler Daniel with Cousin Abigail Jenkins Murray so she could be with Daniel as much as possible. The Murrays' Jack Daw Hall was near their own place, and Cousin Abigail was very much part of the family; not only was her Cedar Grove Plantation near Jenkins Plantation, but Abigail and Daniel were cousins both on their Jenkins side as well as on the Townsend side. Cousin Abigail dearly loved her little Jenkins relative, and the young widow took the child to her heart. And Abigail's own nine-year-old Joseph adored helping care for Daniel.

Hephzibah's second baby was due at any time, and she had counted on being with her husband when the baby came. Hephzibah could not have known, those weeks ago, that shortly after she reached their home on Calhoun Street, the British would arrest Daniel and imprison him in the Exchange Street dungeon. She shuddered as she remembered her last look at him, with British troops leading him under guard out the door. Each day, she sent for word to see how he fared. Each day, old Jack bravely made his way to East Bay Street to find out what might be going on. He moved with great care. Were a British troop to take him on the street, Jack feared the result. The British had a reputation for harsh treatment of slaves. And at night, no one dared appear outside.

Hephzibah recalled so vividly the birth of little Daniel not quite two years earlier. It had not been an easy birth, but there was no one better or more comforting to have with her in such an hour than Maum Jean. She had brought countless babies into the world, both slave and free, and her love and devotion for her Miss Hephzibah was profound.

As Hephzibah inhaled the heady fragrance of the jessamine drifting through the window, she was flooded with memories of her courting days with Daniel. They walked through the gardens at the Frampton plantation, and Daniel occasionally broke off a sprig of jessamine and lovingly tucked it behind her ear. Just the memory of those moments brought tears to her eyes — they seemed a lifetime ago. Hephzibah's thoughts drifted as she remembered how she, as a young girl, had idolized the handsome young man who lived on the Jenkins plantation. For his part, Daniel had begun taking note of the girl at the next plantation when she was about fifteen. Young Hephzibah had noticed him long before that. When he proposed, it was like a dream come to life. And now, here she was, only twenty years old, expecting her second baby, and Daniel was imprisoned in the Exchange Street dungeon. Her heart had never felt more alone and vulnerable.

That sultry Tuesday evening of May 9, 1780, the first labor pain hit Hephzibah; she well remembered the signs from the birth of little Daniel, and whispered to Maum Jean that her pains were upon her. "Never you mind, Miz Hephzibah, you have Maum Jean here with you. You be fine, you be fine now." But the night seemed endless, and the perspiring young mother tried not to scream in pain. Over and over again, Maum Jean bathed her forehead in cool scented water and whispered encouragement through each labor pang.

And shortly before dawn on Wednesday, May 10, there in the basement on Calhoun Street, a tiny newborn entered the world with her first determined cry. Maum Jean cradled the little one in her loving arms before placing the tiny infant in the exhausted arms of her mother. "Miz Hephzibah, you have a little girl, and, oh Miz Hephzibah, she be beautiful, just like her mama!" And for the first time, the wearied young mother gazed with infinite love into the face of her newborn daughter.

"Maum Jean," she whispered, "I'm naming my baby Hephzibah, too. Our name is from the Bible, you know." Maum Jean smiled and nodded. "Maum Jean, it means, 'My delight is in her.'" Then the weary mother looked from the face of her sleeping baby into the eyes of her beloved servant: "Maum Jean, this name also means one who is protected or guarded," she insisted, "and God knows my baby needs protecting!" With that, Hephzibah closed her eyes and fell into an exhausted sleep.

By mid-afternoon of Thursday, Maum Jean's anxiety was

written across her face. Hephzibah's forehead was hot and she moved restlessly. Occasionally, she would be able to hold her tiny baby and give her some sustenance, but things did not look good. Maum Jean had seen the deathly signs of childbed fever too often and felt helpless in the face of what she feared was happening. So often at the difficult birth of a child, fever would set in; even doctors did not seem to understand the cause or how to stem the tide. And there were no doctors to be had. Charleston stood vulnerable to complete collapse at any moment. Bombardment sounded closer all through the day, and Jack did not dare try to get to the Exchange to get news to Cap'n Jenkins.

Tenderly, Maum Jean bathed Hephzibah's forehead with sweet scented water and rocked the fretful infant when she would rouse. By nighttime, the fever was worse and Maum Jean and Jack felt desperate. Brokenly they prayed for mercy and cared for the sleeping infant. Dawn arose on May 12 — and word slipped through the streets like a trail of venom left in the wake of a snail. A nearby neighbor crept out and brought the message: Charleston had fallen. It was totally in the hands of the British. No one was safe.

The next three days seemed an eternity to Maum Jean, bathing the restless, perspiring, anxious Hephzibah and placing the baby in her arms to nurse when she could manage to hold her close. Maum Jean simply tried to keep Miz Hephzibah comfortable, and constantly prayed for mercy. Late on Monday evening, May 15, with tiny Hephzibah just five days old, the young mother looked one last time into Maum Jean's anguished face and feebly clutched her hand. "Maum Jean, promise me. Promise me you and Jack will take my baby home to Edisto. Maum Jean, guard her with your lives. Promise me, promise me!" Distraught, the faithful servant wept as she assured Hephzibah, "Miz Hephzibah, you know we love your baby. We'll guard her. You know we'll protect her, but oh Miz Hephzibah, jus' hang on. You gonna make it; you'll see; you gonna make it."

But Hephzibah knew she was dying. Tears trickled from her weary eyes as she thought of Daniel there in the dungeon, and no way now to get word to him. No way to see him once more. "Maum Jean," the dying young woman whispered, "you tell my little boy his mama loves him."

Both were weeping now. Maum tenderly bathed Hephzibah's forehead one more time and murmured words of comfort, even as she saw the life drain from the beautiful young face. Life was not fair. It couldn't be fair. Her beloved Miz Hephzibah was only twenty years old; she was like the child Maum Jean had never been able to have herself. Surely Hephzibah's life still lay in front of her. But that life slowly, and then with a final, gentle breath, passed into eternity. A weeping Maum Jean and Jack stood by, holding the tiny five-day-old and pleading with God for protection and mercy, even as their minds raced ahead, thinking of just what they must do next.

~ *Two* ~

THE ESCAPE

The tiny baby squirmed in Maum Jean's arms and began to whimper. It brought Maum Jean's awareness beyond the grief of the still form lying in front of her and growing cold, forcing her to focus on what must be done. She and Jack could not leave their beloved Miz Hephzibah lying there; they also knew time was of the essence. Danger lay all around them and they had to hurry. This baby must be protected. They had promised, and the two of them were willing to give their lives to protect her.

While Maum Jean soothed the fretful newborn, Jack made his way up two flights of stairs to the attic. Waving around the small lantern in his hand, Jack found what he was searching for — Miz Hephzibah's dower chest, a beautifully carved piece of workmanship. Swiftly he began removing all the linens stored in the chest. Recalling the lovely silk quilt given Hephzibah upon her wedding to Captain Jenkins, Jack located it in a nearby trunk. It would make a soft lining for this makeshift coffin for their beloved Miz Hephzibah. With supreme effort, he slowly managed to tug the heavy chest down two flights of steps, and then slid it down the final flight into the basement.

Meantime, Maum Jean had soothed her tiny charge to sleep. She hastily found a large piece of soft linen and cut it into squares. Methodically mixing sugar and butter, she placed a dab onto each square of linen. Deftly tying off each square with a piece of string, Maum Jean was able to make a large supply of sugar tits. Many was the time she had used them to soothe Miz Hephzibah herself, when she was a tiny mite. It was precious little nourishment, but under the circumstances, what choice did they have? The consequences of being caught by British soldiers did not bear contemplating. They must prepare to take this baby to Edisto, and they must somehow try to keep her quiet as they fled.

Her work with sugar and butter completed, Jean prepared several jugs of water, some bread and cheese, and wrapped them in towels, tying knots so they could be carried. Jack had the dower chest in the basement by that time and Maum Jean took the beautiful silk quilt and lined the chest, sobbing softly as she worked. It seemed such a short time ago that she had watched Miz Hephzibah place her lovely wedding linens in that very chest, dreaming of all the wonderful years ahead. Those hopes and dreams were lost now, in the cold finality of death.

Tenderly, the old couple placed the body of their mistress in the makeshift coffin and together made their way slowly up the stairs and into the backyard of the Calhoun Street house. The moon was full that May night and gave sufficient light for Jack to see how to dig a shallow grave. Meanwhile, Maum Jean completed her preparations for flight, giving thanks that the baby was still sleeping. It seemed hours before Jack could make the grave deep enough, and somberly the two managed to place the chest in it and cover the spot. Task complete, they stood for just a moment praying, remembering, weeping. And then there was no time for tears — only action.

Weeks earlier, Jack had left their little rowboat in the tall reeds beside the river's edge. Many a time through the years he had paddled the forty miles from Edisto to Charleston and back again, and he knew he could handle the trip. The unknown was the enemy all about them — the danger of discovery by the British. They would have to travel under cover of darkness and hide along the shoreline during daylight. Silently the old couple made their way through the streets of Charleston headed for the river's edge, skirting from bush to bush, remaining hidden at any unusual sound. The heavy fog helped to give them cover and muffled the sounds of footsteps. Maum Jean had used a large linen square to bind the baby to her chest, papoose-style, freeing her hands to grasp the bundles of supplies.

Swiftly and without a word, the two climbed into the small boat and began the long and treacherous journey home. They had to make it. They had promised Miz Hephzibah. The night seemed endless as Jack grew more and more weary from rowing. Each time baby Hephzibah began to whimper, Maum Jean would use one of the makeshift pacifiers and whisper soothing words. And as dawn began to creep across the horizon, Jack found a sheltered cove and steered their little vessel into the midst of tall weeds along the edge of the riverbank. They remained there throughout the day. That first endless day, the two frightened and exhausted slaves dozed and then periodically woke to the sound of marching feet as they heard British accented voices call to one another as troops passed nearby. Each new sound brought renewed and increasing fear of discovery.

On the second night, a sudden squall blew up. Little Hephzibah cried incessantly as the howling wind assailed their ears and rain beat upon the three in the little rowboat. Maum Jean sheltered the child from the cold blasts of rain as best she could, but her resources were pitifully few. Over and over in her frantic mind, Maum Jean repeated the Gullah prayer of her West African people, one she had often heard her own mama pray, calling out, "Oh, Jesus, Jesus, bide in me in a sacred place. Bide here right now." Jack had to stop several times and use a tin bucket to bail water out of the tiny boat. Then, as suddenly as it blew up, the squall blew itself out — and once more hope returned that they might actually make it.

Their harrowing journey took an interminable four days and four nights — rain, fear, boredom, grief and worry were their constant companions. They could not even imagine what poor Captain Jenkins must be thinking — with no way to know how his wife was doing, no way to know if the baby had even been born, no way to be aware of the grave danger surrounding his newborn daughter. There was not a waking minute throughout the dreadful ordeal that the two did not pray for mercy and deliverance, pleading with God to help them save this child.

Maum Jean fretted over having no way to give any sustenance to the tiny infant other than a bit of sugar and butter. How could a baby possibly keep going on so little? On land, they could find a wet nurse and the baby could be adequately nourished; this sure knowledge gladdened the old servant's heart and strengthened her determination. The moment they reached Edisto, they would go to Miz Abigail Murray's, where little Daniel stayed, waiting for his mama to come home. And nearby on Cap'n Daniel's own plantation, Maum Jean's sister's girl, Lily, had just had a healthy baby of her own. Lily would make a perfect wet nurse for this precious little babe. And Maum Jean knew old Mr. Townsend, the patriarch of the Townsend clan and a great-uncle to this tiny one, would turn the place upside down if necessary to save this baby. This tiny mite's own daddy, Cap'n Daniel, was the old man's favorite nephew.

Maum Jean and Jack tried to sleep during the daytime hours, hidden in the reeds and waiting for the protection of night. Maum Jean had too many hours to think and fret, and yet prayer was her mainstay as she pled for God to spare the life of Miz Hephzibah's baby. The exhausted old slave mentally shook her head, thinking back over all that had befallen her dearly loved young missus. Hephzibah's own father, Jonathan Frampton, died when she was just a toddler, not even two years old. He had left her a wealthy child, for she inherited Bleak Hall Plantation. It was a vast holding, but young Hephzibah Frampton was nonetheless an orphan, raised by relatives on Edisto. That little Frampton girl also inherited Maum Jean and Jack, however, and they loved her fiercely and without reserve.

After what seemed an eternity, Maum Jean detected "dayclean" just coming up on the horizon. As a little slave girl growing up on Edisto and speaking Gullah, the language of her people, Maum Jean had always known the early light of dawn as dayclean. And dayclean had never been so welcome as now, for it revealed the shoreline at Frampton's Inlet, very close to Cedar Grove Plantation where Miz Abigail lived. God had answered their prayers and Maum Jean and Jack had kept their promise to Miz Hephzibah. Her baby lived.

Many years later, Maum Jean told the story again and again to Hephzibah, how God had surely saved her life and spared her for a reason. "Chile," the old woman would recount, "by the time we got you home, you was only 'bout fit fuh de fishes!" But live she did, and not just live; she lived to make an impact on countless lives, some near and some a world away.

It was a month later when a weary young captain stood in the prow of a boat making its way through the waters separating Charleston from Edisto Island. Just the week before, a relative had managed to get word to Jenkins at the Exchange Street dungeon that his beloved wife had died after giving birth to their little girl. Hephzibah was forever gone, and the young captain, just released by the British controlling Charleston, was finally headed home to his orphaned children. It had sounded like the baby was still living, according to his cousin Mikell, who had sent him word. Daniel knew nothing of what had transpired, of how his dear one might have died, of how the baby could possibly have survived in the midst of siege and war.

Release from prison could not release the pain in Daniel's heart over the loss of one so dear. He and Hephzibah had a far too brief idyll — falling in love, marrying with high hopes and great joy, welcoming their little son Daniel and anticipating their second baby together. Then it all fell apart, and now Hephzibah was forever gone. He was left with two little ones and they needed him. Jenkins vowed in his heart not to fail this trust, and to raise those babies in a way that would make Hephzibah proud.

Word had gone ahead that Captain Jenkins was finally released and headed home on the ferry that day. As Jenkins stood at the prow of the ship, the outline of those on shore came closer and closer and he could make out the forms of his family members standing on the wharf, awaiting the boat's arrival. And among the shapes, he could soon make out that of the faithful Maum Jean, a little boy at her side clinging to her skirts, and in her arms a small bundle. Daniel Jenkins had come home.

~ *Three* ~

CHRISTMAS 1787
THE GROWING FAMILY

"Maum Jean," pled the young child, "tell me again how you got me home to Edisto. I so like to hear you tell it!"

"Law, chile, you'll wear me out, tellin' that tale — you hear it all the time!" Maum Jean gave her a gentle smile and launched into the oft repeated story: "Shore 'nuff, once upon a time, you wuz a tiny lil' squallin' mite of a baby, jus' born, and I had to keep you lil' mouth stopped up with sugar tits so them British sojers couldn't hear you cryin'." Maum Jean leaned over young Hephzibah's bed to touch her soft cheek and smile into her eager face. "An' my oh my, dat 'ol storm done come up and the winds done blow and dat one night, ol' Jack and Jean thought we shore 'nuff not gonna make it. But chile," she paused and reminisced, shaking her head, "dayclean of de fourth day done long last come; never thought I be so happy to see Edisto smak up in front our lil' ol' boat. But honey chile," she concluded, "you wuz so weak, you wuz so puny, you wuz only 'bout fit fur the fishes, shore 'nuff."

The old woman leaned back and looked up toward the ceiling, thinking back to that epoch morning. "Missy, God dun got somepin' special in mind for you; why else He dun spare yor lil' life? And look at you now!" she shook her head back and forth in wonder, "purty as a lil' picture. You jus' like yor sweet mama I done raised — an' you good as gold, too, jus' like her."

Seven-year-old Hephzibah sighed with satisfaction. She never tired of hearing how God indeed must love her for He had surely spared her life. She might be only a child, just a girl at that and tiny for her age, but nothing was small about her heart and will. Sometimes Papa would look at her and get the strangest look in his eyes. Then he would smile and tell her how like her beautiful mother she was — same shining black curls, same deep-set black eyes, those speaking eyes that seemed to look right into a body's soul — and then conclude by reminding her that she was smart like her own dear mama as well.

Indeed, Daniel Jenkins often felt a pang of the heart when looking at certain expressions on the face of his young Hephzibah. She was so very much like her mother, his first love. Not that he didn't care for gentle Martha, his new wife. She was uniformly kind and tender with the children. Sometimes though, she appeared quite unsure of herself and hesitant about making decisions. Martha was a distant and slightly younger cousin; she and Daniel had grown up together, with Martha idolizing her handsome older cousin. Martha had herself been raised by a stepmother and keenly remembered how it felt to have lost her mother when very young. Daniel Jenkins had been released from prison not long after Hephzibah had been born and, needing a mother for his two little ones, had married Martha. Thus, it was that Martha suddenly found herself the mother to two small children. And then, sure enough, not a year had passed before the young matron gave birth to a babe of her own.

The newly forged Jenkins family had already experienced their share of tragedy, but this was not unusual; such was the case with most of their neighbors and relatives as well. Disease or war or an accident could change their lives in a moment. Martha had been so delighted when baby Mary was born the year after they married. Hephzibah and her big brother, Daniel, were every bit as excited and doted on their baby sister. But then the winter of 1784 brought terrible influenza. Tiny Mary developed a severe case and did not have the strength to recover. All too soon the toddler was just a memory. Daniel Jenkins recalled the stricken look in Hephzibah's eyes and how he had tried to reassure her time and again that her beloved baby sister was now safe in heaven with Jesus.

He was also aware that Hephzibah and her brother had an unusually close bond, playing and learning together, each dependent on the other. The two referred to each other as "Sister" and "Brother." Jenkins smiled as he thought of how having so many "Daniels" in the family could be confusing to the children. Not only were father and son both Daniels, but the family patriarch, Daniel Townsend II, claimed the same name. The elder Daniel had for years been master of a nearby cotton plantation and had only recently died at the ripe old age of eighty-four. To further compound the confusion, the old gentleman's son, Daniel Townsend III, still lived on the Townsend place. Daniel III was a frequent visitor at the Jenkins place, so "Daniels" abounded.

Life had a comfortable rhythm to it of late. Martha slowly recovered from the loss of little Mary and last year gave birth to her first son, Benjamin. Benjy was a healthy, strong toddler and loved to follow his elder siblings around. It was difficult for him to sit still during morning prayers at the breakfast table, and the toddler usually fell asleep during family devotions each night. Hephzibah and Daniel both liked taking turns reading from the big family Bible at family devotions time, proud of their ability to read just like Papa did. The children were especially excited just now, for tonight they had helped read aloud the Christmas story, with this favorite holiday just around the corner.

The older children attended Edisto Episcopal Church with their parents each Sunday and learned to listen quietly, although they found the services interminably long. Hephzibah seemed to have an unusually profound sense of the reality of God in the world. Possibly it came from her hearing the oft-told tale of how God was responsible for having spared her life. Whatever the reason, she was surely mature beyond her years.

Martha at times seemed almost younger than her little stepdaughter, and gladly turned over to Hephzibah any of the household duties for which the child showed an aptitude. Daniel had explained to his daughter that one day she would be responsible for running a large plantation, for her own dear mother had named this child her heir. Hephzibah Frampton herself had been quite an heiress, inheriting from her father, Jonathan, the vast property known as Bleak Hall, a large land area covering much of the southern section of Edisto Island. It was Hephzibah's wish that this inheritance would go to her daughter.

The child was eager to learn the mechanics of running a large home, and clearly had an excellent tutor in the form of the devoted Maum Jean. That keen old servant was just as devoted to this Hephzibah as she had been to the child's mother. Jack was growing old now, but remained a font of practical wisdom on the

Jenkins place. Quite spry for his years, Jack was a general factotum around the house and plantation, and all the servants relied on his great good sense. Daniel Jenkins could never be grateful enough to the old couple for literally risking their lives in order to keep their promise to "Miz Hephzibah" and save her baby girl.

Maum Jean was the unspoken leader of the household help, and no one quite dared to go against her wishes. The servants seemed to have developed their own hierarchy and community on the Jenkins plantation. Nearly all had come from the Angola area of West Africa, bringing with them much of their culture and way of family relationships. In a departure from many of the slave-owning families both on Edisto and indeed throughout the low country, the slave families on the Jenkins plantation were not broken up and sold.

Daniel had learned from his own father, Richard, a sense of regard for those under his care. The very idea of slavery was a constant problem for Jenkins. He had grown up with it as a way of life — men owning men. However, it always bothered him, as it had his father before him. Certainly, their livelihood depended on the labor of the slaves, but Jenkins's conscience forever had trouble dealing with the whole concept. Something of the contradiction of the entire system constantly nagged at him, and it appeared that this sense of the unfairness of things as they were had conveyed itself to his young daughter. Hephzibah was keenly sensitive to the feelings of others and clearly looked on Maum Jean and Jack as part of her family.

Daniel remembered watching his father deal with the vagaries of plantation life in his day. Slavery had come to Edisto over a hundred years earlier, when cotton had become such a dominant crop. Increasingly, cotton demanded more and more labor. Richard Jenkins had felt the burden of owning another human being and had never felt comfortable with it. Daniel had followed suit, but realized that the great majority of his relatives and neighbors simply took slavery as a necessity. It made their own prosperity possible. Owning slaves was a reality of life that disturbed Jenkins — and Hephzibah, young as she was, reflected a similar attitude. Daniel Jenkins privately applauded her valiant young spirit but foresaw the day when she would have trouble dealing with the callous opinions of friends and the like, who certainly didn't think in accord with Hephzibah's standards. She might be just a seven-year-old child, but she displayed a sense of justice far beyond her tender years.

For his part, Daniel Jenkins suspected that his daughter's democratic tendencies were fostered not only by her fierce love for Maum Jean but also by the children's English governess. Like many of his wealthy neighbors, Jenkins had hired a tutor/ governess for his children, particularly to prepare his son to attend university. He didn't adhere to what many of his fellow plantation owners felt, thinking that an education was wasted on girls. Jenkins wanted his daughter to have a solid foundation of learning to equip her for the role of plantation mistress that would certainly be hers. His hired governess, Evelyn Bekins, was young and idealistic, the younger daughter of an English vicar who had educated his children himself. Miss Bekins had come to the newly independent United States to support herself and to embrace an adventure that would challenge her mind and spirit. It appeared that this spirit, as well as her intellectual capabilities, was already giving her young charges a sound base on which to expand their minds.

"Beekie," as the children affectionately called her, was quite a strict disciplinarian, but took pains to be fair. In addition, the young governess had a keen sense of humor that appealed to her pupils. She might also be something of a revolutionary, for the thought of slavery offended her sense of justice and no doubt she communicated these radical ideas to her young pupils. Only hazily aware of the tutor's unconventional philosophy, Jenkins was thankful for her skills in mathematics and geography and her love for the classics; his son would certainly be ready for university in a few years. As for Hephzibah, she was like a sponge, absorbing both knowledge and attitude in the nursery classroom.

And in just days, it would be Christmas; the children were already excited. One of their favorite things was the giant Christmas oyster roast, with all of their friends and neighbors getting together for an all-day outdoor celebration. The children loved the excitement of playing with scores of young friends, their shouts mingling in the air with the fragrance of roasting oysters and wild boar barbecue on the outdoor spit. Young Hephzibah's favorites were the sweets, dainty individual servings of sweet potato pudding and abundant platters of piping hot gingerbread. The celebration lasted all day, with the children falling into bed in happy exhaustion. Daniel and Martha helped Maum Jean tuck them in that night, sending them to bed with the news of a Christmas present that would be coming in the new year: another baby brother or sister. Hephzibah gave a contented sigh and sank into sleep with thoughts of a new baby on whom she could lavish her abundant affections.

Four

SUMMER 1790
SUMMERS IN CHARLESTON

The summer following Hephzibah's tenth birthday had arrived; along with spring, it was her favorite time of year. She and Brother loved the warm and scented air, with flowers bursting into bloom all around and the fragrance of jessamine and orange blossoms filling the air. The riotous colors of azaleas in varied hues of pink and fuchsia vied to catch the eye. Hephzibah found their beauty second only to that of the giant live oaks that bent their branches over the driveway leading up to their plantation. The long and curving avenue of oaks, each garlanded with wispy gray moss, seemed to smile a welcome to anyone visiting the Jenkinses. Hephzibah never tired of gazing up into the tangled limbs of the oaks and wondering how many years they had stood there, watching life pass up and down the road over which they stood sentry. Brother told her that her imagination was way too vivid — trees couldn't watch anything. To the whimsical young girl, however, they seemed to be smiling down on her.

This afternoon, Hephzibah was going to Aunt Abby's in the small children's cart she and Brother used when they visited neighbors and family. Their fat old pony Jezebel couldn't be hurried. Jezebel earned her name at a very young age, being exceptionally uninterested in heeding commands. The passing of

the years had slowed down her stubborn streak a bit and Jezebel
had come to terms with her young masters.

Aunt Abby was close to Hephzibah's heart. The young girl
always looked forward to these afternoons when Aunt Abby
taught her special quilting skills. Of course, Abby wasn't really her
aunt, for she and Papa were double cousins, since they shared two
grandmothers — both Grandma Townsend and Grandmother
Jenkins. Aunt Abby was dear to Hephzibah. When her mama was
in Charleston, back when she was born, Abigail Jenkins Murray
was the one who kept Brother. Then when Maum Jean and Jack
brought newborn Hephzibah back to Edisto, it was Aunt Abby
who took care of her until Papa got out of prison. Back then,
Abigail was a young widow, her husband being an early casualty
of the War for Independence. She raised her small son Joseph and
managed to run their thriving plantation, Cedar Grove, with real
competence. When Aunt Abby remarried, this time to Ephraim
Mikell, she moved to Blue House Plantation. Cousin Joseph was
twenty now, and in charge of Cedar Grove.

Abigail cherished a special love for the little girl who had been
brought home half dead and looking too frail to possibly survive.
But make it she did, and Abigail still got tears in her eyes thinking
of that day when Daniel Jenkins saw his tiny daughter for the
first time. Not having a daughter of her own, Abigail lavished her
affections on Hephzibah and adored passing on special feminine
skills to her. In turn, Hephzibah found in this intrepid woman a
splendid role model for learning how to run a household as well
as how to manage a busy plantation. Since Blue House Plantation
was close to the Jenkinses' own place, visits to Aunt Abby were

a treat to be anticipated just about every week. Aunt Abby knew precisely how to design appliqués for quilts and how to properly place intricate quilting stitches in a straight row. A needle was like a hummingbird in her hand. Hephzibah was fascinated with the process and ever eager for a new challenge to her developing skills. There was always too much to do to ever become bored.

Going to Charleston was on Hephzibah's mind as she headed home from Aunt Abby's this hot summer afternoon. Papa was a state senator and his duties often took him to Charleston. Young Daniel and Hephzibah particularly enjoyed those times when they were allowed to go with him. Charleston meant lots of relatives who enjoyed indulging Daniel Jenkins's two children who had so early lost their mother. There were Mikells and Whaleys, Jenkinses and Townsends, Capers and Adamses, and other kin as well.

The children sometimes visited with family at St. Philip's Episcopal Church, but their favorite times were Sundays when their Mikell relatives took them to Charleston's First Baptist Church. The Jenkinses' Charleston house was on Church Street, conveniently close to the Baptist church. Just three years earlier, a new young pastor had come from High Hills to take up his duties there. Richard Furman was a favorite with the youth, and his daughter, Rachel, became a special friend of Hephzibah's. Rachel was three years older, but something about the keen mind and winning personality of the young Jenkins girl appealed to Furman's daughter, and the girls regularly corresponded. The Furman home was just a couple of blocks up Church Street from the Jenkins place, so visiting was quite convenient. Hephzibah was planning a new letter in her mind as she headed home that afternoon, deciding just what news she would write to her friend Rachel.

Papa's senatorial duties were quite intriguing to a child with the broad intellect of Hephzibah Jenkins. Jenkins told the children about the excitement of the day just two years earlier when he had been able to sign the document by which South Carolina ratified the brand new U.S. Constitution. It sounded like an important part of their newly founded republic, and Hephzibah was proud of the fact that her father was actively involved in setting up the new government. She wished girls could do things like that. However, never being one to waste time on what couldn't be, Hephzibah instead contemplated just what things she could manage to accomplish herself. Surely girls and women were important, too, and her fertile mind was always plotting just what she might do that was significant. It did not occur to her that it was highly unusual for a girl to have such an interest in the affairs of state going on around her. The keen influence of a rather unusual governess might well have something to do with fostering such an interest, to say nothing of a father who was closely involved in the young nation's government.

Feeling helpless was a condition that was anathema to a child with the force of character of Hephzibah Jenkins. A drive to action seemed to be an innate part of her personality. Just the week before, on her way home from Aunt Abby's, the ten-year-old had noticed a commotion out in the cotton field of one of the neighboring plantations. With horrified eyes, she watched as an overseer repeatedly whipped an elderly man who couldn't keep up the pace of his hoeing. The child's face had flamed with anger, and she hastened home to corner Papa and tell him what she had witnessed. Daniel Jenkins's heart sank as he read the rage on his daughter's face — and when she burst out with, "Papa, can't you DO something about that?" he could only heave a deep breath and explain to Hephzibah that he had no right to interfere with his neighbor's methods of handling his slaves. "Sister," he tried to explain, "this is a free country, you know. Our neighbor has the right to do what he wishes."

Hephzibah was incensed. "But, Papa," she burst out, "that doesn't make sense. That old man working in the field lives in this country, too, and he doesn't get to do what he wishes." Jenkins had no answer for such logic. His mind knew it to be true, but current reality did not concur. As best he could, he simply assured this child that on the Jenkins plantation, such a thing would never be allowed to happen. That was a promise. With this, Hephzibah had to be content, but whenever she saw some act of callous cruelty, the determination in her heart to do something about such injustice grew apace.

It was surely unusual for a child in the low country at the end of the eighteenth century to develop such a view. Hephzibah had taken to heart the message she had heard all her young life. Surely God did have a reason for saving her life; she was determined to find that reason. The day after she had seen the whipping of the slave, it was still on her mind when Maum Jean tucked her into bed. From long practice reading Hephzibah's face, Maum Jean shook her head a bit and inquired, "Somepin botherin' you chile. Tell old Maum what 'tis." And out came the incident that had fretted Hephzibah's thoughts all evening, as she related the events of the cotton field. "It just isn't right, Maum Jean. That is so cruel!" "Yeah, Honey, it not right," the elderly servant agreed, "but it happen anyways."

"But Maum Jean, why should just the color of your skin make you a slave?" the child persisted. "Honey," Maum Jean sighed, "this ol' woman don't have no way a knowin'. Jus 'tis. But chile," she continued, "my body might be a slave, but my mind ain't." She paused and added: "Even a slave got a piece a' God's ear. He somehow always hep us make it through." And with this, her young charge had to be content. Nevertheless, Hephzibah filed away in her mind the events of the day, and, with the tenacity of a dog with a particularly appealing bone, she just couldn't quite let it go, tucking it away to be worked on another time.

With the time drawing closer for the trip to Charleston, Hephzibah completed her missive to Rachel Furman and began a second letter to another particular friend, Eliza Pinckney. She and Eliza were the same age. Both had been born in Charleston, and both their papas had been among those South Carolina leaders who ratified the new U.S. Constitution. In fact, Eliza's papa was part of the important Constitutional Convention in Philadelphia that actually wrote the document. Hephzibah found this impressive. Furthermore, Eliza, too, had lost her own mama and had a stepmother. The two girls looked forward to the times when Hephzibah could be in Charleston, and they could talk and visit and formulate plans for their futures. The Pinckneys' town residence was just about two blocks away on Meeting Street, and the girls managed to find frequent opportunities to get together.

Hephzibah realized that this Charleston house was not the

one where she had been born that May night in 1780. Papa still got a haunted look in his eyes when someone mentioned the siege of Charleston and his time in prison. His sensitive daughter understood that the memory of the death of her own mama still burned in his mind, as he recalled how he had not even been able to be there with her. That house had held too many memories. This new house of the Jenkinses' on Church Street had been something of a fresh beginning for the grieving young captain.

Attending services at First Baptist was never boring for the young girl. Pastor Furman had started something new this year for children at the church, and Hephzibah was eager to visit and be a part of it. He had just instituted the Juvenile Missionary and Education Society, and Hephzibah was anticipating becoming part of the group. Rachel had written that the Society was learning about how to help the Catawba Indians learn about God. Hephzibah knew from experience that just hearing Rachel's father talk was something special — no boring long sermons with Pastor Furman. He always seemed to know how to tell Bible stories that made the characters come alive. Rachel Furman had written that the youth in the group were actually gathering offerings that would go to help Indian children. The idea had appeal for the dreamy young girl who constantly seemed to be searching for a worthy cause to champion.

Maum Jean normally did not go on these trips to Charleston. With so many dependent on her varied skills around the plantation, she was nearly always needed on Edisto. Hephzibah especially missed Maum Jean when bedtime came. Her beloved Maum always had a fine story to tell, and Hephzibah loved a gripping tale. She was storing up in her capacious mind the treasure trove of ancient lore that Maum Jean was passing on. Much of the elderly woman's storying came from tales she herself had heard through the years, tales handed down from one generation of slaves to the next. The fact that the Frampton and Jenkins slaves had been allowed to remain in family units had strengthened the core of cultural knowledge passed down from parent to child year after year. The culture of Angola, so reflective of that part of West Africa, was quite distinctive with patterns of family relations highly important, and the language they had developed in the New World was distinctly their own. It mixed somehow into a creole of various African tongues, coming to be known as Gullah. It would prove to be long-lived.

Hephzibah had heard Maum Jean use her own mixture of words so often that the child was quite adept at understanding what was being said by the slaves speaking Gullah around the plantation. She loved such expressions as *buckra* ("the white man") or *kubba*, the Gullah word for "cover." Hephzibah's quick ear caught the nuances of tone and she could sound just like Maum Jean, who spoke of "de peacha dat taak frum de Holy Book." She learned that "brother" was *um*, for Maum Jean grinned and told her, "U iz fa um, yu brodda him be." To Hephzibah's quick mind, Gullah was somewhat like learning French from Miss Bekins, who spoke it so precisely, informing her that every young woman needed the accomplishment of speaking a second language. Hephzibah felt quite confident that now she spoke not just one, but two other languages.

Papa had indicated that on this Charleston trip, just he and the older two children would be going. Martha and the younger children would be remaining on Edisto, as Martha was not feeling very well. Benjy was four years old now and in rapid succession, Martha had given birth to two more sons, Thomas and Richard. Hephzibah had not gotten her earlier wish for a little sister. Now Martha was increasing yet again and Hephzibah was earnestly, if secretly, praying, "Dear Lord, this time, please let it be a girl!"

Five

"It's a girl!" Hephzibah still smiled every time she thought back to that chilly November morning two years earlier when she and Brother bounded down the steps in response to Papa's call to come quickly. There Papa stood at the bottom of the staircase, a tiny bundle in his arms. Her eyes shining with joy, Hephzibah reached out and, without a word, Papa carefully placed the precious bundle into her eager arms. It was love at first sight. Brother bent over the tiny baby, and he and Hephzibah gently pulled aside the swaddling blanket, inspecting each tiny finger and counting every little toe. Hephzibah looked up at her father and breathed, "She's a girl? You are sure?" Daniel Jenkins smiled in response, "Oh, yes, it's a girl, Hephzibah. At long last you have the baby sister you longed for."

Baby Sister had a name nearly as long as she: Amarinthia. Always older than her years, Hephzibah had from that moment taken this child to her heart and lavished love upon her. Martha, gentle and somewhat diffident in personality, was quite willing for this older child to spend as much time and effort on her cherished new sister as she wished. It was the beginning of a singular bond that would last a lifetime. Amarinthia shared a closeness with her sister that was to enrich both of their lives. As soon as 'Rinthia was able to take her first steps and toddle around, she was her sibling's faithful shadow, absorbing from this idolized older sister much of Hephzibah's perspective on life. An already busy and active young Hephzibah merely found a way to accommodate time for baby Amarinthia into her bustling daily schedule. It became a familiar sight around the Jenkins plantation, the quicksilver Hephzibah moving from house to garden to neighborhood with little sister tagging along right in her shadow.

Upon the arrival of this longed-for little sister, Hephzibah wrote to Rachel Furman to share the news. Rachel had written earlier in the year with news of her own. The Furman family circumstances had altered considerably in just one short year. Rachel had become fast friends with another young woman who attended their church, Dorothea McDonald. "Dolly" had a birthday one day after Rachel's, and although Dolly was her senior by four years, their friendship was quite close. The relationship changed in quite an unusual way, however, when Rachel turned twelve. The day following Rachel's birthday, Dolly had had her sixteenth birthday, and just a week later, she became Mrs. Richard Furman. Now Rachel's friend was her stepmother! It was a massive change. Nonetheless, the relationship's shift did not affect their friendship, and Rachel learned to adjust to having a stepmother scarcely older than herself. Hephzibah had been amazed to receive the letter telling of the wedding. The next year Dolly had a son, and Rachel a new half brother, only slightly older than Hephzibah's new sibling. There were frequent letters between Edisto and Charleston about the joys and challenges of being elder sisters.

In the ensuing two years, Hephzibah and Rachel had

been able to share both correspondence and time together, as Hephzibah made the trip to Charleston several times each year. When the Jenkins family arrived in Charleston the summer of 1792, Hephzibah was able to renew her companionship with Rachel, and the two of them remarked again on the similarities of their lives. Now the girls had one more commonality: another sibling. Hephzibah's half sister Martha had arrived in the spring, the namesake of Hephzibah's stepmother, Martha.

Soon Hephzibah would be in her teen years and she was gaining increased skills in all areas of her life. Daniel Jenkins noticed a deepening seriousness in his oldest daughter's outlook on the world. He realized she was already dreading when Brother would go away to college; their tie was closer than that of most siblings, and it would be a wrench for his daughter not to have her beloved big brother at home. Jenkins suspected that his daughter wished that girls, too, had such an opportunity. There was certainly no lack of intelligence on her part; the constraints on her gender were a factor that often frustrated this young girl who evidenced such depth of character and an eagerness to be doing things both useful and worthwhile.

Also much on Hephzibah's mind was her relationship with God. When at home on Edisto, she and Brother faithfully attended weekly services at their Episcopal church. The liturgy was familiar to Hephzibah, but she somehow left Sunday worship with a certain sense of emptiness, thinking that there must surely be something else. She and Brother were quite familiar with Scriptures; after all, the family had evening devotions, and it was a comforting part of every day's routine. However, it was in the worship services in Charleston that Hephzibah felt most alive and challenged, as she listened to Dr. Furman explain passages from the Bible. He was a gifted speaker, and his word pictures made Scripture and its truths seem to leap to life for her. During that summer of her twelfth year, she realized her personal need for saving grace. In later life, Hephzibah referred to Christ from that point on as her Polar Star.

However, this decision of Hephzibah's heart presented something of a dilemma to her seeking mind. She had been sprinkled during a confirmation service by their Episcopal minister shortly after her birth. When she listened to Dr. Furman, and as she read about baptism in the New Testament, the young girl puzzled over what she read. Nonetheless, she decided that this could be a matter to mull over in her mind, determining later how best to handle this concern. The newness of Hephzibah's relationship with Christ was a quiet joy that she cherished in her heart, and there was about her a new sense of calm resolution that permeated all she undertook to do.

Charleston turned quite miserably on the brazier of summer that year of 1792, and Hephzibah was not disappointed to go back to Edisto and catch a bit of breeze under the ever-present live oak trees. If one stood at just the right spot, one could feel a breath of air off the water at Frampton's Inlet and it cooled one nicely. Part of Hephzibah's problem was that she was nearly always too busy to stand still long enough to cool off. The faithful Maum Jean was aware that her beloved "chile" was developing rapidly, while at the same time she herself was growing more and more frail. Maum Jean felt an urgency to pass on her bits of wisdom and ways of getting things done to this one around whom her own life had revolved.

Hephzibah was nothing if not intuitive, and she silently observed the signs of frailty that were gradually affecting her beloved Maum Jean. That resolute woman saw to it that Hephzibah was aware of what went on around the Jenkins plantation and gently directed her in learning how to deal with the reality of their plantation world, master and slave, on a daily basis. Maum marveled at the way a twelve-year-old could view life through eyes far more mature than many adults, a young woman who illustrated bone-deep integrity and instinctive empathy in her dealings with others. Maum Jean also frequently observed that some of Hephzibah's peers, whether cousin or neighbor, occasionally resented her bossiness. The young girl was never one to vacillate. If she saw something that needed doing, she simply acted, even if it was not a popular decision. "Force of character" was a phrase that would aptly describe the rapidly maturing young Miss Jenkins.

Thanks to Maum Jean, Hephzibah was familiar with all aspects of plantation life. Occasionally, she and Brother walked to the fields and observed how the crops were planted, sown and harvested. She also scrutinized the work that went on in the milk house, the way the truck garden provided vegetables for the family table, and the way the little slave children were cared for in the nursery area. In point of fact, that was one of her favorite spots. Hephzibah would take little 'Rinthia with her, and the two would play with the babies and toddlers there. The little ones clambered around Hephzibah and hung onto her skirts as she would teach them little songs and nursery rhymes.

Here, as in other areas of the plantation, Maum Jean's watchful care had made sure that baby care was handled properly. Several of the older women worked in the nursery, using one of the rooms as a sleeping area, the other for eating and playing. Hephzibah enjoyed watching the little children who were a bit older, helping to care for the babies and toddlers. 'Rinthia delighted in their times in the nursery and often begged Big Sister to let her stay longer.

Always in the back of Hephzibah's mind, it seemed, was the thought that these little children were precious souls just like those in the big house, and the discrepancies in the quality of life between these little ones and her own siblings was an ache in her heart. Why was it this way? She had no answer. There was one comfort for her, however, as she puzzled over this conundrum. At least at the Jenkins plantation, these slave families were allowed to stay together. It never ceased to chill her blood to think of the countless families where mothers and their babies were torn from each other's arms and sold, never to see one another again. The young woman vowed in her heart that this would never occur where she had some say.

There was no place on the plantation, though, that lured Hephzibah more than the large kitchen, that fragrant kingdom ruled over by Jane. This was the only name Hephzibah had ever heard for her, just Jane. The head cook was a force in herself and had been in charge of the kitchen as long as Hephzibah could remember. Jane didn't look quite like the other slaves, for she was a mulatto. As a small child, Hephzibah had asked Papa why Jane's face looked different, and he had explained that Jane's father had been a white man. Jane had grown up in New Orleans but had been at their plantation for as long as Hephzibah could remember. Jane's hand with biscuits was nothing short of magic, and each of Jane's cakes was a masterpiece. When in a good mood, Jane would allow Hephzibah to have a hand in the mixing, and the young girl marveled at the deftness with which the cook could turn out perfect pastries and mouth-watering entrees. Evidently she had picked up special skills in New Orleans, for many of her dishes displayed a French flair. Daniel Jenkins was the envy of Edisto for the excellence of his table.

Another of Hephzibah's favorites in the house was Grace; this young woman was Maum Jean's sister's granddaughter, and Maum Jean had trained her from the time she was tiny in just how to run a household. No speck of dust dared linger where Maum Jean's eagle eye could detect it, and Grace followed in her great-aunt's footsteps. Grace had "jumped over the broom" last year with William, and now their first baby was soon to arrive. Hephzibah had frequently observed the wedding ceremonies of a number of the slaves living on the place, and knew that they first had a religious ceremony with the minister. The custom, however, was to follow the formal vow-taking with a "broom-jumping." All agreed that this brought good luck. On their wedding day last year, first Grace had jumped the broom, then William. A wedding celebration had followed, with plenty of food and dancing for all the slave population at Jenkins Plantation.

Now Hephzibah was excited because Maum Jean was predicting that Grace's baby was coming at any time. Among her numerous skills was midwifery. Maum would be right there to engineer the event when Grace's little one decided to arrive. Once more, Hephzibah was hoping for a girl; it just seemed that there were always more boys being born, and this time she was counting on another girl.

It appeared good fortune was smiling on them, for on one late September evening, Maum Jean came to Hephzibah's room with a wide smile wreathing her face. She had never forsaken their time-honored custom of bedtime prayers together, and Maum Jean's face was invariably the last that Hephzibah saw each night. This night the old retainer arrived with news: Grace's baby had arrived, and that baby was a girl child! Now Hephzibah beamed and immediately wanted to know the baby's name. "Bella, honey chile," Jean informed her. "She one beautiful baby and her name Bella." And Hephzibah Jenkins went to sleep in great contentment over the thoughts of baby Bella, anxious for morning to arrive so she could see the tiny infant. Hephzibah could have no way of knowing the way that her life would intertwine with that of this newborn slave child, and how each would bless the other down through the years.

~ *Six* ~

SUMMER 1793

GROWING UP

The long, hot, drowsy, lazy days of summer were upon them, but the lazy part of the depiction of life in the summer on Edisto would never match any description of young Hephzibah Jenkins. The lively teenager never seemed to have enough hours in her day. Little 'Rinthia managed to keep up with her big sister much of the time, and Grace's tiny Bella had become an important part of Hephzibah's daily routine. She could not quite explain the pull on her heart this young slave child had become. Her development was of intense importance to Hephzibah, and she and 'Rinthia found time each day to play with the winsome toddler.

Maum Jean felt a tug at her own heart as she watched the way her young Missy poured herself into this little slave girl; indeed, just about anything Hephzibah did was with this kind of whole-hearted fervor. Bella was a little mimic, picking up with ease words and phrases from 'Rinthia and Hephzibah and sounding like a little Jenkins herself. All three loved to watch Jane in the kitchen, and if the little ones stayed out from under her feet, she was tolerant of their presence and didn't mind to hand out a cookie here and a choice nibble of one of her mouth-watering desserts there. Jane had no children of her own; normally, she didn't have time to waste on little ones, but 'Rinthia was an exception, and for some reason young Bella seemed to have quickly won her affection.

Maum Jean's mind was already thinking ahead, deciding that Bella might just find her special skills in the kitchen, especially with someone like Jane to teach her. That was far ahead, however; Bella was just now toddling on her own and getting into everything left within her reach. Most slave children would never have been allowed the latitude afforded Bella. But then most such children did not live on the Jenkins place and have a special position in the good graces of Miz Hephzibah.

In like fashion, Hephzibah was also picking up traits and characteristics she saw in the lives of those closest to her. In turn, those nearest to Hephzibah were noticing the way she was quickly maturing, leaving childhood behind and stepping into young womanhood quite rapidly. The soft curves of her face were taking on a new refinement, with clear-cut cheekbones and arresting eyes that seemed to always look just beneath the surface and see what was really there. A penetrating look from those fine eyes could either lift a heart or make one uncomfortable about what those eyes might be discerning below the surface. The striking young woman with the shining black curls and graceful carriage was garnering attention from young men on various plantations around Edisto, to say nothing of a number in Charleston who saw her at family gatherings or when visiting with friends following Sunday services.

Hephzibah herself seemed oblivious to this newly awakened attention; she was too busy with all the things that captured her imagination. In the course of life on the Jenkins place, or visits to Aunty Abby's, or time spent with relatives during the week, her own personality was giving an indication of the ways in which these important others in her life were helping to shape her own philosophy and beliefs. Most were positive influences; a few were not. Hephzibah appeared to have a built-in method of discerning hypocrisy or callousness. These would quickly fire her temper, and Daniel Jenkins had time and again reminded Hephzibah that her highly developed sense of justice and what was fair and right just might one of these days get her in trouble.

In fact, the troubles and triumphs found in Jenkins family lore were often the topics on the evenings when the family gathered after supper for devotions and family time. Of course, family stories were not just stories of the Jenkinses but also included their myriad related families — the Framptons, Whaleys, Mikells, and, with certainty, the Townsends. Hephzibah and Brother had reached the conclusion that practically everyone on nearly all of Edisto's plantations was related to everyone else. Hephzibah's favorite evenings were the frequent ones when Cousin Daniel Townsend came for supper and lingered on during the long summer evenings to chat and reminisce over old times. Cousin was a great storyteller, and Hephzibah and Brother were enthralled by the yarns he would spin about kith and kin from years gone by.

The lure of the tasty meals that came from Jane's kitchen were in themselves enough to attract their relative, but since the death of his father, Townsend particularly relished the company of relatives with whom he felt so much in common. Since Cousin Daniel's father was actually Jenkins's uncle as well, the two men had always felt a close bond of kinship, and in point of fact were quite close in age. Hephzibah and Brother especially enjoyed hearing Cousin relate the tales his own father had passed on to him of their mutual ancestor, Daniel Townsend I, who had moved from Massachusetts to Charleston for warmer weather and new prospects. The Massachusetts Townsends were related to Governor Winthrop of the Massachusetts Bay Colony and had been prominent early citizens. Daniel I, being the sixth child, had decided to make his own fortune in the South, having heard intriguing stories about the thriving city of Charleston.

Daniel had gone on to become a city leader, prosperous businessman and landowner, and an elder in the Independent Congregational Church, with its distinctive circular building. The Jenkins children were particularly intrigued with the details of their great-grandfather being on the jury selected to try the "gentleman pirate," the notorious Stede Bonnet. Hephzibah got delicious chills just thinking about that pirate who had made his prisoners walk the plank. Bonnet, for a while, even became partners with that most infamous of all the pirates, the legendary Blackbeard. Actually, Cousin Daniel reminded them, their great-grandfather was only able to help bring Bonnet's *men* to justice, for the Gentleman Pirate himself escaped, only to be recaptured a few months later and hanged right there in Charleston.

Not ghoulish at all, but certainly closer to home, were the stories Cousin shared about his beautiful mother, Susannah Harrison Winborn, whose family hailed from Virginia. Susannah had died just months before Hephzibah's birth, so she had no memories of this great-aunt of hers. She did recall her great-uncle Townsend however, with his snowy white hair and the way he enjoyed bouncing her on his knee, tweaking her shiny black curls.

Great-uncle Townsend had a long white beard that tickled when he kissed her cheek.

As Cousin Daniel told about his mother Susannah, it was difficult for Hephzibah to picture her as a beautiful young fifteen-year-old bride, for Daniel III's father had been all of thirty-eight when they married. Papa assured her, however, that Susannah had been a radiant young mother and a gracious hostess. In point of fact, she had just been a few years older than Hephzibah's own papa. "But it seems to me," Hephzibah commented, "that she was marrying someone really old!"

Cousin Daniel, regarding her closely as she made this observation, added a thought, "But then, Hephzibah, they loved each other very much. That was easy for anyone to see."

Hephzibah sighed a bit, "I just wish I could have known Aunt Susannah. It appears to me," she continued, "that oftentimes you see a younger bride, but just about never a younger groom." Cousin Daniel started to respond, but then appeared to think better of it, for he quite abruptly changed the subject. Hephzibah's curiosity was aroused by this diversion. She had been around Cousin all her life and thought she knew him quite well. At the moment, however, Hephzibah was silently pondering about what he had nearly said. Cousin was the sort of person who gave away his thoughts as gifts. It could be difficult to know just what he was thinking. She stored the puzzle of the missing comment in the recesses of her mind, to be pulled out and mulled over at a later date.

Cousin turned the direction of the conversation by asking Papa about his childhood memories on Edisto. Papa's own mama had died when he was very little. Grandfather Richard had then married Martha Rippon. Grandma Martha had subsequently raised Papa along with her own children, and upon Grandfather's death about twenty years earlier, had run the plantation on her own, and most competently at that. Hephzibah had overheard various relatives referring to Grandmama as "a regular old brimstone," but she had never been anything but indulgent with Daniel's little orphaned daughter. Actually, Grandmama's youngest daughters had still been at home when Hephzibah was born. The three of them — Elizabeth, Ann and Sarah — had doted on their little niece. Hephzibah had been around Grandmother Martha enough to observe in her a force of will combined with a sense of justice that impressed itself on the mind of a little girl who was just learning about her world. When Papa told stories about his childhood, it was plain to see that everyone had had a special role to play in the family, and if you failed on your part, Mama Jenkins soon let you know how to remedy the situation. Several decades had taught Captain Jenkins not to court the edge of Mama's tongue, but he also developed that same observant eye she possessed and not much missed his scrutiny.

On the other hand, Hephzibah's own stepmother, Martha, shared the same name but was a real contrast in personality. Ever self-effacing, Mother Martha was nonetheless invariably courteous. She never commanded you to do something, but somehow, when she looked so diffident and worried, you wanted to please her and carry out her wishes. Martha Jenkins was a study in gentleness, and Hephzibah realized how soothing that could be when life got trying, which it so frequently did. Her stepmother's genuine kindness had a way of disarming people; it often made

Hephzibah think of the old adage Maum Jean liked to use: "Honey chile," she'd say, "you catches a lot more flies wif honey 'dan you does with vinegar!"

Papa loved to tell about the olden days when the Framptons and Jenkinses had been neighbors and when different branches of the family were establishing plantations in assorted locations around the island. Papa made sure Hephzibah understood that since she stood to inherit the vast property that came from her own mother, she needed to understand the land and how to be a good steward of this inheritance. From the earliest years, the child realized that she had a job in life and it was important that she learn how to do it well.

Actually, learning special skills from Aunt Abby was a favorite and painless way to prepare for the responsibilities that would one day be hers. Along with the needlework expertise of Abigail Murray Mikell, Hephzibah was finding out how this resourceful woman ran her plantation household.

Hephzibah especially found the process of designing and crafting quilts fascinating. As she and Aunt Abby work on a quilt for Hephzibah to put in her hope chest, Abigail talked about the beauty of using quilts to help record a family's history. "Building a quilt, my dear," Abigail told her young protégée as they worked together on the tiny stitches that formed the picture, "is a bit like building your life's story. The stitches tell the tale for a future generation to see and experience what touched *your* life."

Hephzibah had been fascinated by the hawk owls that proliferated around the Jenkins plantation, so she and Aunt Abby had designed a beautiful small quilt that captured the hawks' wild beauty. Hephzibah smiled inwardly, thinking about some young girl centuries later, seeing this quilt and wondering about the girl who told the story of the owl. The many hours spent with Aunt Abby had been the informal classroom in which Hephzibah had learned lessons from life that were illustrated by Abigail herself, this woman who coped with what life threw her way with real grit and a regular dash of humor as well.

Hephzibah's imagination soared when she heard how Aunt Abby's husband, Joseph Murray, had been helping defend Edisto from the British when he was killed by an exploding cannon. Uncle Joseph was intensely patriotic, and Hephzibah was a bit surprised to learn that, years earlier, certain of the plantation owners on Edisto maintained loyalty to Britain. This made for some antagonism even between relatives; several of the Loyalists had left, but others remained and came to terms with being part of the new Republic.

The young girl's intense sense of patriotism made it difficult to understand how anyone could feel anything but devotion to the principles of free America. She recalled some interesting discussions with her former governess, Beekie. Miss Bekins was British, yet quite broadminded in her outlook on freedom. But then, the governess came to the newly minted United States because she had an adventurous heart, and soon she lost her heart to a young American and married him earlier in the year. Hephzibah and her brother missed Beekie's stimulating classes. It would soon be time for Brother to head off to college, however, so a new phase of their lives was about to begin. Hephzibah, who never did anything by halves, was already looking forward to the future and dreaming about what might be just around the corner.

~ Seven ~

1794-1795
THE TRANSITION YEARS

The little black-haired child with delicate features highlighted by compelling dark eyes had more than fulfilled the promise of beauty that fond family members had once predicted for her. Hephzibah was a strikingly lovely young woman who often displayed a quiet dignity in her words and actions, but just as frequently showed flashes of playfulness and a subtle sense of humor, including that quite rare talent of being able to poke fun at herself. The many older slave children around the plantation were often heard telling some obstreperous boy or girl, "Better watch out! Missy Hephzibah'll likely scald you with them eyes!" Numerous young ones had learned to think twice before picking on someone younger and smaller, for surely Missy would take up for weaker ones.

Everyone on the plantation looked up to Marse Jenkins, admiring his integrity and respecting his word as law, yet when they looked to his daughter they looked for an extra dollop of fairness and mercy. With Missy, you knew you would always get a fair hearing. In point of fact, family and slave alike could see reflected in Hephzibah many of her father's traits. He was consistently fair, and his daughter had learned that lesson well. From Jenkins, Hephzibah picked up not only her keen patriotic streak but also her papa's conflicted response to slavery itself. Daniel Jenkins grew up with slavery as a way of life, but certain friends in Charleston like Henry Laurens had further impacted his thinking. Laurens was one of the largest slave owners in South Carolina, but ended up freeing those in bondage to him and declared more than once that he abhorred slavery. Jenkins did not free his slaves, but he had not forgotten the impact of Lauren's one short searing phrase: "I abhor slavery." Daniel Jenkins never personally resolved the issue, yet never was he to be without this contradiction nagging at his heart and conscience. Hephzibah grew up with this inner conflict affecting her world. She did, however, end up handling it in a way that reflected the depth of heart and that sense of justice that permeated all she did. It was a way that was quite unique in the South of the eighteenth and nineteenth centuries.

Hephzibah's personality had as many layers as a French pastry, and her cousin from the Townsend plantation often noted her in action. Daniel Townsend observed her defense of the underdog on frequent occasions and watched those speaking eyes stop a quarrel in mid-flow. He often sensed as well a special camaraderie between Hephzibah and Brother. He heard them jump to each other's defense time and again. Their uncommon bond reached back to the earliest years, possibly from having lost their own mother so early. Townsend vividly recalled his first sight of Hephzibah more than fourteen years earlier, when the exhausted Maum Jean arrived at Cousin Abigail's door holding the tiny babe who was so frail and close to death. He smiled as he contrasted that memory with the vibrant, sparkling young face of his cousin now.

Townsend had been at the Jenkins place this evening when Hephzibah took little 'Rinthia out to the milk barn to introduce her to the new litter of puppies residing there. He grinned as he watched young Bella running after 'Rinthia and her beloved Miz Hephzibah. Daniel's keen eye saw the tenderness with which the teenager treated both children and smiled to himself to see her face reflect the innocent joy in the faces of 'Rinthia and Bella. This young woman, he reflected, and not for the first time, could be tender yet tough as well.

Daniel had no doubt that much of her instinctive response to injustice or cruelty came from her fierce love for the woman who had saved her life and helped to mold it. To Hephzibah, Maum Jean, enslaved as she was, still walked with a dignity that spoke volumes about her character. That remarkable dignity in a woman who had been a slave all of her life had somehow crept into the makeup of the young woman she had saved and cherished. Surely, Townsend thought, no one has had a greater influence on this lovely young relative of his who was just now reaching womanhood.

This particular August afternoon, Townsend came to talk with Hephzibah's brother Daniel, who would soon be leaving for college. After visiting with young Jenkins, he had discovered Hephzibah with the little ones at the barn. As they watched the children playing with the puppies, Daniel discussed Brother's eminent departure for university. Townsend wondered how she was handling the impending departure of her closest sibling. Young Daniel was headed to Princeton, and to Hephzibah, New Jersey sounded like a foreign country and just about as inaccessible.

She realized the time must come, but that didn't make it easier. Hephzibah had expressed herself on numerous occasions, (and expressing herself was something that came easily to her) that she surely wished girls could have that kind of education, too. This girl was always one, though, to make the best of whatever could not be changed, and she continued to dream dreams of what she might one day be able to do. It never dawned on her that she might one day be the person God would use to start a movement that would involve women in worldwide service.

It was in fact those dreams of Hephzibah's that were of special interest to Daniel Townsend just now, for he had been contemplating for quite some time now a change in his relationship with this young woman. Her words a year earlier about his mother having married an "old man" had given him pause for concern, because Daniel Townsend had grown to love the vibrant young lady now walking at his side. He had always cherished and adored this cousin, of course, but in the past year, his feelings had deepened and grown. He hoped against hope that he could win her heart. In fact, the previous year he had talked seriously with Daniel Jenkins about his daughter and how his feelings for her had been growing apace. Jenkins, at first somewhat shocked, realized upon reflection that Townsend had in more recent months been around the Jenkins plantation even more than usual. This might be the reason behind his frequent visits.

Jenkins listened to his cousin lay out his case, and agreed that he could give his blessing if Townsend were willing to wait for a year or so before making his feelings known to Hephzibah. Furthermore, he advised Daniel that the decision would strictly be up to Hephzibah, and cautioned him that she might balk because of the great difference in their ages. Townsend, well aware of the obstacles in his path, was enough committed to this possibility that he was willing to take the risk. At least he knew that Jenkins did not consider him a fortune hunter, for Daniel III was a wealthy man in his own right. But he was discerning enough to realize the size of the task that would be his in winning her heart. He had seen on all too many occasions that young Hephzibah Jenkins had a mind of her own.

Furthermore, Townsend was a realist, and her comments about the young bride and the older husband often came to his mind. It would be much the same for Hephzibah and himself. After all, he had been twenty-one years old when she was born. However, he saw the deep love between his own older father and younger mother and knew that genuine love made the difference. At the same time, Daniel was aware of the force of will that characterized Hephzibah Jenkins. He was not blind to the challenge before him. Their differences were not only the disparity in age. Daniel was an elder in Edisto's Presbyterian church and he well knew Hephzibah's leanings toward the Baptists. In fact, she often brought up the subject of having a Baptist church there on the island again, as there had been a century earlier. Daniel certainly knew her well enough to understand that she would very likely not be interested in becoming a Presbyterian.

Moreover, he was already well into his thirties and liked to be in control. Townsend was also most astute, seeing very clearly that Hephzibah was not only headstrong and loyal, but also very willing to express her opinions. Daniel the suitor understood the need to tread softly and was even going to have to summon up enough courage to know just how to initiate a courtship. He was all of thirty-five years old, but had never been serious about a lifelong relationship.

This golden autumn afternoon, Townsend walked back to the house with Hephzibah. After the children ran off to the kitchen, he suggested that the two of them walk over to Jacob's Well, which stood near the big woods. As they walked down the winding curve of the driveway, the oyster shells that covered the drive crunched pleasantly beneath their feet. Daniel quizzed Hephzibah about her knowledge of island lore and talked of tales of a century earlier, when the somewhat mysterious William Mellichamp developed a thriving business by manufacturing salt here at Botany Bay, and had a monopoly on its sale all through the Province. Bleak Hall — this vast stretch of land covering much of this side of Edisto Island — had its share of legends, dating back to when the Edisto Indians had lived on the land and hunted in its forests, leaving bits and traces of their presence behind. Hephzibah was especially fond of speculating about Jacob's Well, nestled close to the bridle paths running near the big woods. That long-ago Jacob had carved on the tabby walls of the well, in Latin: *Jacobus fecit.* Hephzibah had always wondered about this Jacob who said he "made it."

Cousin Daniel could spin a fine yarn, and he described stories of long ago when countless young lovers had trysted on the spot where they stood and sworn undying love. The top of the well was steeple-shaped and Hephzibah could only speculate on how long it had stood there. Cousin grinned and reminded her that a little gray man was supposedly always standing on guard to keep the water pure, even if you couldn't see him. Hephzibah smiled up at Daniel, hearing this piece of nonsense, and noticed how the sun made his clear brown eyes appear to have hazel depths in them. She had always taken for granted his clean-cut features, determined chin and the strength inherent in his tall frame. As usual, a lock of shining brown hair had fallen across his brow, looking for the world like an upside question mark — she always itched to take her fingers and tuck the curl back in place.

Then voicing the question that popped into her mind, she asked, "Cousin, have you ever met someone special here at Jacob's Well? And," she paused, "why is it you have never married?" As Hephzibah looked into the familiar face of her cousin, she noted for the very first time something more than kindness in his eyes. Townsend, taking in a deep breath, decided he might as well make a start at this thing. Having had no experience in courtship, it did not come easily to him. *Strange,* he thought to himself, *I have never really even considered such a serious step before.* Then gazing with tender eyes upon the glowing young woman who had been growing up practically in the same family with him, he reached out to take her chin in his fingers: "Hephzibah," and he hesitated, "maybe it's because I've been waiting for someone to grow up." For a moment, the young woman looked puzzled and then high color flooded her cheeks. "Me, cousin — are you talking about *me?*" Townsend smiled quite tenderly and gently flicked one heated cheek with his finger. "Yes, Cousin, you are exactly right. You. However," he hastened to explain, "I'm not going to rush you. No doubt this is something of a surprise to you."

"A *surprise?*" the young woman responded. "More like shock!

Me?" she questioned again. "You mean me?"

"Oh, yes," Townsend replied, and with a gallantry Hephzibah had never experienced personally but only read about in fictitious tales of love and derring-do, Daniel reached down and lifted one dainty hand to his lips, gently kissing it. Again the color flooded Hephzibah's cheeks. It was one of those rare moments when she was speechless. That hardly ever happened to Hephzibah Jenkins, and Daniel was amused to see the astonished look in her eyes. "Come," he lightened the atmosphere, "let's head back for supper. I wonder what magic Jane has wrought in the kitchen?"

As they started back down the path leading to the Jenkins home, a late afternoon sun was touching the land on its way to sinking in the sky with shades of blue mingling with evening red and gold, then touching the ebbing tide in Botany Bay. "And don't fret," he reassured her as they walked toward the house, "I'm not wanting to rush you. Take your time and think about it. But," he emphasized, "I'm serious about this. Very serious, my dear and cherished cousin."

~ *Eight* ~

1795
THE COURTSHIP

Hephzibah sat at her desk, penning a letter to Rachel Furman and relishing the quiet of her room and a break from all the noise and clutter of the day. Her desk was one of her favorite spots, a bit of a personal oasis when she needed some quiet time. She stroked the surface of her delicate Louis XV desk, with its shiny marquetry and the cunning little drawers set in two rows across the back. These were the places where she tucked her favorite treasures, her correspondence from Rachel and Eliza in Charleston, and now the letters from Brother at faraway Princeton. She had sensed a bit of homesickness in his most recent letter, but accounts of some of Brother's activities on weekends and with his friends gave hope that he was adjusting. It crossed her mind that her letters full of all the minutiae of life around the Jenkins plantation might make Brother long even more for home. Somehow she was hesitant to fill her letters with the subject so frequently occupying her mind these days, her time spent with Cousin Daniel and the change that was forming in her relationship with him.

Hephzibah discovered it was difficult to call Cousin by his given name, even in her thoughts. But then, this was the habit of a lifetime, and it made her a trifle shy to stop the word as it came out of her mouth and change the "Cousin" to "Daniel." Practice was helping however, and loath as she was to mention him very frequently in her letters to Brother, she did not feel a similar constraint when writing to Rachel. Yet another common strand in her friendship with Pastor Furman's daughter was the interesting fact that both were in the midst of their first serious courtship. Hephzibah felt free to write of the feelings of her heart to this friend who would surely understand what she was experiencing.

"My dear friend," Hephzibah wrote, "I take pen in hand to inquire how life is progressing in Charleston. I have been quite busy since our return from the city, and I am convinced you are more than busy yourself, what with all the duties of daily life in the Furman household. I am guessing that by this time you have another little halfbrother or sister! Your stepmother must be so very grateful for the valuable assistance you render to her so faithfully. And, Rachel," Hephzibah smiled as she dipped her pen again into the inkwell to her right, "I am all agog to learn the newest chapter in your promising friendship with the dashing Mr. Thomas Baker. I recall meeting him when I last attended services there in August. I found him most refined and, clearly, he had eyes only for Miss Rachel Furman. Has your father made any comment to date on this interesting development?"

Hephzibah sat for quite some time, deciding how to disclose to her friend what was happening in her own life with a certain suitor. "You may be a bit surprised to hear that I am pursuing something of a similar interest myself. Likely you recall me mentioning our cousin Daniel Townsend who frequently spends his evenings with us. It develops that he is very interested in me becoming something more than his cousin. I must admit,"

Hephzibah paused again and wondered how to explain this strange new development, "that I was shocked when Daniel first intimated that he was seeing me with new eyes. You see, Daniel is a full two decades my elder, and at first I felt that surely he must be jesting. But no, Daniel is quite serious. He approached Papa before ever speaking to me about this interest; however, Daniel assured me he wants to give me time to think about this. I am hoping, Rachel," Hephzibah smiled to herself as she continued, "that soon I may have the pleasure of introducing Daniel to my dear friend Rachel Furman. He has a house on the corner of Tradd and Meeting Streets, so when in Charleston he is quite close to our home there on Church Street, just a block or so away."

"Nonetheless," and Hephzibah paused at length as she puzzled over just how to express her thoughts, "I must consider several things when thinking of the future. I admit to being somewhat gratified that a few young men have expressed an interest in securing my attention, but also confess that I have not been inclined in any of their directions. Daniel is indeed much older, yet I find that we have much in common. But," and again Hephzibah thought through her words, "there are a few points that I feel need close attention."

"Daniel is an elder in Edisto Presbyterian Church, and dear friend, you know my Baptist leanings. This might prove a problem, although I have read many times that love conquers all. Do you think this is just a truism, or maybe has some validity? I may find out, if this courtship proceeds! I am also pondering the difficulties that could be involved in marrying *anyone*. The realization of the prevailing custom that when a bride marries, her husband has control of all her inheritance, is presenting something of a problem to my thinking. You see, Rachel," Hephzibah smiled a bit before proceeding, "although Daniel has told me that one of the things he most admires about me is my 'force of character,' I am wondering if he will still admire my force of character when it comes up against his own will. You can see the struggle going on in my mind. My friend," she concluded, "it helps me so much to be able to bare my heart to you and know that you will understand. Please let me know how Mr. Baker and you are progressing. I am most interested. Your affectionate Edisto friend, Hephzibah."

She had thought to write a note to Eliza Pinckney as well, but the hour was growing late so Hephzibah hastened to get to her evening duties. 'Rinthia needed tucking up, and Hephzibah had promised baby Martha a bedtime story as well. Since dear Maum Jean was likely to be helping with bedtime, Hephzibah did not doubt that little Bella would be with her, hearing the stories along with Hephzibah's young sisters. The beautiful little slave child Bella had a firm hold on Hephzibah's heart, and she often wondered just what might happen to her in the years ahead. Tiny though she was, Bella was already developing remarkable skills around the kitchen. Jane not only tolerated her presence, but also seemed to delight in passing along skills to the little girl. Heading to the children's bedroom, Hephzibah was thinking about their comfortable nightly routine. Each evening, as was their custom, Hephzibah and Maum Jean guided the children in their simple prayers, establishing an important ritual that the young woman hoped would last a lifetime. Hephzibah's reliance upon the Lord was deepening with the years, and in her heart of hearts she always looked to her Heavenly Father as her Polar Star.

Several days later, Daniel Jenkins returned to the house after a busy morning around the property, handling all sorts of situations that arose in the course of a normal day. This day was a bit out of the ordinary, however, for Daniel Townsend had ridden over to talk with him about a serious matter. Townsend had decided the time had come to approach Hephzibah with a proposal, but most properly, he wished to make certain yet again that this was agreeable to Daniel Jenkins. After all, this was his beloved eldest daughter. Jenkins had been watching for several months now, bemused by the progress of Townsend's interest, as he observed his careful interactions with Hephzibah. In spite of his age and obvious maturity, courtship was something new to Townsend and he was treading new water. The two men had spoken frankly, and Jenkins assured the younger man of his approval, but cautioned him that in no way could he speak for his eldest daughter. She most decidedly had a mind of her own.

This was not news to Townsend; he had watched this captivating young woman grow and develop and had observed her determined spirit in relationships with many on the island, whether an older relative, a peer or a servant. There was no question about her intelligence or depth of character. Nor was there any doubt about her strong will. It was very evident. Hephzibah was fifteen now, and Daniel thought it time to bring this courtship to a start. Confessing to himself an inward trepidation, Townsend chose this particular afternoon, with a late summer sun just sinking enough to let the air begin to cool off, to take courage in hand and make the plunge. Finding Hephzibah just crossing the door leading to the parlor, Townsend asked if she had time for a short walk.

Nothing if not perceptive, Hephzibah smiled in agreement and sent word to her stepmother that she would be back in time for supper. Again Daniel chose the setting of Jacob's Well, and it afforded the two of them a bit of privacy. In the house, one never knew who might come walking into the room. Townsend had rehearsed in his mind many times just what he might say, but it all became a jumble in his mind as they drew close to the well. A bit of cool shade provided by a stately and venerable live oak tree near the well provided a fitting setting for the anxious suitor. "Hephzibah," and Daniel cleared his throat, "I want to ask you something." Smiling up at her cousin, Hephzibah noticed the little tic at the side of his mouth that always seemed to twitch when he was nervous. And he was nervous just now. As he looked down into the deep-set dark eyes in the piquant face that had become increasingly dear to him through the years, Daniel reached for her hand, holding it gently as he told her what was in his heart.

The words began to flow out, as he expressed how deeply moved he had been on numerous occasions as he had observed her staunch sense of justice in defending those who could not defend themselves. He spoke of the way he had seen her love for children and the gentle manner in which she protected and guided them. "And yes, my dear Cousin, I am very aware of your force of character. I know full well you do not hesitate to speak up for what you think is right and just." Hephzibah's eyes flashed a bit, and Daniel smiled and added, "But I am also very aware of your quiet dignity, and how it can sometime turn to impish fun as you look on the bright side of things."

"My dear Cousin Hephzibah," Daniel took a deep breath and continued, taking her face between gentle hands and tilting her face up to his, "I so much want that quiet dignity and sense of justice to be part of my life. Would you do me the honor of being my wife?" Daniel rushed ahead before she could respond: "And I would promise to love and cherish you all the days of my life."

"Daniel," Hephzibah replied with shining eyes, "do you think you can endure my force of character? Oh, I do hope so," and she paused and took a deep breath, "for you are very dear to me." Daniel responded with a massive smile of relief, and, taking her left hand in his, slipped onto her third finger a beautiful ring with a ruby, surrounded by a circle of gleaming diamonds. As he closed her fingers around the sparkling ring, he breathed as if a prayer, "And thus, I plight you my troth."

There was much merriment around the supper table at the Jenkins plantation that evening as Hephzibah and Daniel shared their news. Jenkins himself was not the least surprised, but gentle Martha was somewhat bemused at what seemed to her a sudden change in the household. 'Rinthia tried to get her mind around the idea of her beloved Hephzibah getting married and setting up a separate home of her own, and three-year-old Martha had no understanding of the import of this big family news.

Townsend and the Jenkinses talked through some practical ideas about when the wedding might take place and all agreed that next spring, when Hephzibah was at least close to sixteen, would be an appropriate time. Hephzibah's heart was full of all sorts of new thoughts and emotions. There was so much to sort through in her life. There would be enormous changes, many adjustments, so much to be done, but already she was dreaming about just what the future might hold. Of one thing she was convinced: Daniel would be at her side, and life would never be dull.

~ *Nine* ~

APRIL 1796
THE WEDDING

Excitement, trepidation, a sense of joy, and a touch of uncertainty all warred for space in Hephzibah Jenkins's thoughts and emotions as the wedding day drew nearer. In the months since Daniel had proposed, the two had spent many hours talking about their future. Hephzibah was aware that their ideas didn't always march hand in hand, even though their bond of closeness was moving to a new level. It still took getting used to for Hephzibah to think of herself as mistress of her own home and likely the mother of children. In her daydreams, she could see a chubby little boy toddling around, looking much like his father with chestnut hair and keen blue eyes. Daniel had a smile of singular sweetness, and this little toddler in her daydreams smiled in that same precise, engaging way. By the same token, Daniel himself could imagine a dainty little girl child with sparkling black eyes and raven curls, a miniature of her mother.

In point of fact, Hephzibah had precious little time to spend weaving air castles. There was far too much to get done. Much on her mind was the situation here at home. Over the years Hephzibah had assumed more and more of the responsibility for the daily running of the house and realized the difficulty that would be afforded her gentle stepmother when she left home. Not only was Hephzibah herself soon to depart, but Maum Jean and Jack and some of their relatives as well would be part of the move. There had been a tacit understanding that where Hephzibah went, Maum Jean went. The elderly servant had been "family" since the days when Miz Hephzibah's own mama had been a baby girl. The wise old woman considered herself a "Frampton." Furthermore, Maum Jean was increasingly frail, in her seventies now and suffering from arthritis. Old Jack was even more fragile and moving more slowly all the time. Both needed less responsibility, not more. Daniel Jenkins had never let fade the depth of his gratitude to the old slave couple who had saved the life of his child. Hephzibah was particularly pleased that young Bella would be moving with her, for that child had a special spot in her heart. It had been this way since the night of her birth.

The bride to be was concerned as well about her little brother and sisters; others would have to step up and help Martha Jenkins in guiding their care. Of course, Papa was a mainstay for her siblings, so Hephzibah felt satisfied that they would thrive. She felt a special wrench to her heart, however, to think of not being with 'Rinthia every day. The clever child was six now and bright as a new penny. Hephzibah comforted herself with the thought that she could have 'Rinthia over frequently and still be an important part of her life. Their unusual closeness had simply grown through the years. And no doubt she would likely have little ones of her own very soon. The thought did not shock her; Hephzibah had been helping raise babies since she was still a mite herself, and nurturing babies seemed to come naturally to her.

When Hephzibah had written Brother with news of the

engagement, she discovered in his letter of reply that he was not really shocked. Daniel Jr. possessed perception to a great degree himself and had not missed the signs of Townsend's increasing interest in Sister prior to his leaving for Princeton. Brother had been home at Christmas and soon would be returning for the wedding. He appeared to relish the idea of Daniel Townsend being not only his distant cousin and friend, but a brother-in-law as well.

Throughout the winter, Hephzibah and her fiancé spent frequent evenings in the parlor after family devotions and getting the little ones tucked up. There was so much to discuss. Where should they live? What crops would be the best to grow? Should they build a new house? The number of practical matters to discuss seemed endless, but that was part of the fun of dreaming about the days ahead. Hephzibah was less comfortable when the talk came around to settlements, handling funds, making decisions. No fool she; the customs of the times and the laws of inheritance were common knowledge. That did not prevent Hephzibah from chafing at the thought of Daniel being legally in control of her inheritance. Had she been born into a modest little home, this would have afforded no problem. That was not the case. Hephzibah Jenkins was an heiress of note. Knowing that Daniel had followed tradition and talked with Papa about her inheritance and about providing for her every need did nothing to lessen her displeasure with both law and custom.

On one of their protracted evenings in the parlor, Hephzibah went so far as to give a hint of how she felt. Most brides, she commented, seemed fine with the idea that their husbands would control all money and property. However, Hephzibah frankly

acknowledged that she was not one of those. Daniel was clearly
ill at ease when discussing such a topic. His preference was to just
let it be clearly understood that he would always provide for her
every need. Secure in his love, Hephzibah did not doubt Daniel's
sincerity. What she did doubt, however, was her own ability to
handle the problem gracefully. When these discussions grew a bit
tense, she would notice the nervous tic in Daniel's cheek begin to
twitch. That always seemed a good indicator that this was the time
to simply bite her lip and move to a safer topic of conversation.

On the other hand, the two were both eager to talk about
plans to build their own new place. For the time being, Daniel
wanted them to live in the Townsend plantation home. As soon
as possible, though, he hoped they could build on Hephzibah's
property. That piece of land had long been known as Bleak Hall.
The property dated back to 1710 and her ever-so-great-grand-
father, John Frampton, so it had a feeling of family and perma-
nence about it. Its location near the shores of the Atlantic Ocean
would make a fine setting for a plantation home. Daniel was
equally excited about the prospect of planting much of the land
in the new Edisto crop, Sea Island Cotton. The island's soil had
proven especially suited to this type of cotton. Sea Island Cotton
was already bringing a premium on the European market, and
between all of Hephzibah's land, plus Daniel's — both on Edisto
and on neighboring Wadmalaw Island — they would have an
abundance of space for growing the prized crop.

Of less import, but more immediacy in Hephzibah's mind,
were actual plans for the wedding. She wanted to follow tradition
with something old, something new, something borrowed,

something blue. Her beautiful ruby and diamond engagement ring had belonged to one of Daniel's grandmothers, so that took care of the old. Those lovely new satin slippers she had chosen for the occasion covered the new. Realizing that the "borrowed" item was supposed to be lent by a woman who was happily married, a pair of Aunt Abby's kid gloves would be the very thing. As a finishing touch, there were delicate blue flowers embroidered on the trim at the bottom of her wedding dress, so Hephzibah was delighted with her bow to tradition.

She and Rachel Furman had exchanged frequent letters in the months since the engagement. Rachel had become engaged to her Captain Baker just weeks after Hephzibah's surprise announcement and now to the delight of the friends, they were both getting married during the same week in April. It was likely that Rachel and her Thomas would soon be moving upcountry to the Sumter area but surely they could continue to correspond. Hephzibah found Rachel a great sounding board for her ideas and hopes, secure in the knowledge that Rachel would never laugh at her thoughts or reveal her secrets to anyone. Such a friend was a treasure.

Aunt Abby was a great help in carrying out plans for the wedding; Hephzibah's Hawk and Owl quilt that Aunt had helped her make several years earlier was now part of her hope chest, along with some beautiful soft linen garments Aunt Abby had prepared and trimmed with lace. Even 'Rinthia had painstakingly made a sampler for her adored big sister. It lay in the hope chest, a labor of love by a six-year-old; the much-worked-on little sampler had crooked but legible letters forming Hephzibah and Daniel's names, with a rather endearingly lopsided depiction of two hearts intertwined, and bearing the date April 9, 1796. The child had begun her work of art soon after hearing of Sister's coming wedding and had spent countless hours bringing it to completion. Hephzibah treasured the sampler far more than all the intricately embroidered work and lace on the many soft lingerie pieces lying nestled in the chest.

April and the wedding drew nearer each day. It was always late at night, after all the tasks of the day were complete, that Hephzibah's thoughts were free to return to the questions gnawing at her peace of mind. She would go to bed exhausted, yet her mind continued to race as thoughts fought each other for consideration. In her heart of hearts, Hephzibah did not doubt that Daniel truly cared about her. But could she gracefully handle the fact that he would be making all their decisions about money and land, choices by which she would have to abide, whether or not she agreed? And this was money, this was land, that she had personally inherited. That deep sense of justice that was such an intrinsic part of her personality rebelled at the idea. Hephzibah would lie on her bed, trying to picture problems that would likely arise, chewing on the corner of her lip as she thought about how she might handle all of this. Surely God was going to have to give her some special grace. But then, her mind would shift to a dreamlike state where all problems seemed to have a way of fading into insignificance when covered by love. Didn't love conquer all? And usually, right in the middle of trying to figure out a happy-ever-after ending, she would fall asleep before the conclusion could be reached.

April 9 was fast approaching. It was still one month until Hephzibah's sixteenth birthday, but Papa had agreed that it was "close enough." Most girls did not marry until the age of twenty or older, having first "come out" for a year or so. Hephzibah was not most young women, but one quite unique in both maturity and understanding. Something about the force of her personality determined that no one who met her would soon forget the young lady with the flashing dark eyes and beautiful smile. Jenkins had laughingly informed his soon-to-be son-in-law that he likely would soon realize that his choice for wife was a force of nature. The thought of conflicts in personality were something Townsend didn't spend time dwelling on. He doted on this radiant young woman and was in a haze of happiness as the wedding date approached. It could not come too soon for him.

As for Hephzibah, the details all needed putting together: the completion of the beautiful cream silk dress with its stylish drop front and the sleeves of three-quarter length with their fall of delicate lace. Being short of stature and having a fine boned build, Hephzibah's fashion sense informed her that she didn't need to be overwhelmed with frills and furbelows. Furthermore, simple yet elegant suited her sense of fashion. She planned to wear her hair loose, and caught back with a creamy fresh camellia from the plantation gardens. Her only attendant would be young Amarinthia, who had been bursting with excitement for weeks about being in Sister's wedding.

The bride with Baptist "leanings" would have loved to ask Dr. Furman to perform the ceremony, but with no presently existing Baptist church on the island, and with Furman's own daughter to be married just days before, she abandoned that idea. Daniel was an elder in Edisto's Presbyterian church and was also president of the board of the corporation and a leader in the congregation. The two had decided that the wedding would be held in the parlor of the bride's home that Saturday morning of the ninth, and they would ask Reverend McLeod, Daniel's pastor, to perform the ceremony.

Surely half the island claimed kin to the Jenkinses and Townsends, and those gathered for the morning ceremony spilled out into the hall leading into the parlor. And to the back of those gathered for the ceremony, with hands quietly folded and eyes gleaming, stood Maum Jean and Jack. Maum Jean's eyes glistened with tears as she watched the beloved child of her heart and Massa Daniel exchange vows to love and to cherish.

During the simple and sacred ceremony, Daniel and Hephzibah pledged their love and devotion to each other until death did them part. Hephzibah watched through a blur of tears as Daniel repeated the solemn words of Reverend McLeod while placing on her finger the wedding ring and pledging his love and devotion in the name of the Father and of the Son and of the Holy Spirit.

The wedding breakfast — with the traditional rich spiced bride's cake, served with strong cups of coffee and the consumption of hard cider — was a festive time that April morning at the Jenkins plantation. Jane's magic touch in the kitchen ensured that the wedding breakfast could not be equaled anywhere on Edisto Island. Early in the afternoon, while family and friends lingered to celebrate the occasion, the new couple departed on the ferry for their wedding trip. Hephzibah and Daniel Townsend could not know that this was to be the beginning of a union that would touch and influence countless lives far beyond their own generation.

— *Ten* —

1798-1799
THE NEW FAMILY

The late evening breeze coming in the open window was listless, filled with the sultry humidity that is such a part of summers in the low country. As May crickets sang their lazy evening tunes, Hephzibah sat rocking little Daniel and crooning to him one of the Gullah tunes that Maum Jean had sung to her so many times. That seemed a lifetime ago, mused the young mother who had just passed her eighteenth birthday. Those same ancient tunes that her dear Maum Jean sang to soothe her little charge years ago lulled the next generation to sleep on this sultry night. Hephzibah treasured these quiet evening moments with her firstborn. The days had a way of filling up and overflowing, going from task to task, and times like this were the cherished moments — all too fleeting. The words were calming as she quietly crooned, "I been walkin' de road long time, O Lawd, n' I not weary yet."

Daniel was growing rapidly and was a big boy for a fifteen-month-old. Hephzibah was especially conscious of his weight on her lap since another baby was due any time now and she didn't have much of a lap left. She smiled to herself, remembering how she had frequently hoped for a baby sister years ago, and how boys had always seemed to outnumber the girls. Now 'Rinthia, that longed-for baby sister, was nine years old and no longer a baby.

In fact, 'Rinthia and Hephzibah had both welcomed another baby brother within two months of the birth of her own small Daniel, so this baby's uncle was the younger of the two. At least that baby was a "Joseph" so there was no name confusion. At the moment, Hephzibah was miserably tired, waiting in the oppressive heat of an Edisto Island summer for her second child to be born.

Always one to rise to a challenge, the young Mrs. Townsend had taken to motherhood as a natural. That first year of marriage passed in a whirl, the wedding trip barely over and work begun on their new plantation home, when the telltale signs of morning sickness struck with a vengeance. As was the custom of the day, women did not speak openly of such things, but Maum Jean was a treasure of wisdom. For one who had never had a baby herself, she still knew more than anyone on the place about birthing babies.

Those first months of marriage had held constant adjustments for Hephzibah. They still did. In fact, it seemed to the strong-willed bride that there was something new to work through just about daily. In her mind, Hephzibah labeled these disagreements as *domestic discomforts*. Daniel was generally a quiet man, but he was long used to making unilateral decisions, seldom feeling the need to ask his wife's opinion. This was a challenge for a young woman with the force of character of Hephzibah. It cut against the grain to not have her opinion valued, and there were frequent fiery discussions between the two — always ending, however, with temporary resignation on the part of at least one and renewed determination on the part of the other. One fact remained strong, and it was not just the force of habit: There was a clear bond of love building on a strong foundation. But even on the days when

Hephzibah despaired of getting Daniel to even listen to her point of view, she did not doubt his love. That assurance worked as a soothing balm.

For his part, Daniel never ceased to be amazed at the inventiveness and ingenuity of his young bride. He respected what he had observed of her character even as a child, but to actually allow her to help make plans and have a voice in decisions was another matter. So long had his own opinion been the only thing he needed to consider that his marriage to a strong woman was a challenge. How could he ever have thought that marrying a young bride would mean that she was still malleable, especially if that young bride was named Hephzibah? In spite of frequent confrontations (for want of a better word), time lent depth to Daniel's appreciation for the keen mind his beloved possessed. Hephzibah might be young in years, but sometimes she exhibited a wisdom that belied her youth.

And Townsend doted on the baby, his little namesake. He could not imagine life without his young family. The new little one was due within weeks and, along with Hephzibah, Daniel, too, was hoping for a girl. Both were hoping that the new home would soon be finished, for the family was likely to continue to grow. Building proved a time-consuming endeavor, even with all the help they had from servants in the construction of the immense house. A number of the slaves were skilled with woodwork, and Bleak Hall, as they intended to call their new home, would be a fine structure. Daniel indulged Hephzibah's fantasy and planned a little cupola to grace the top of the three-story mansion.

Hephzibah's friend Rachel had written with the momentous

news of the birth of William, her first son, about four months after Hephzibah's baby had come. The two young mothers wrote regularly, exchanging news about each new milestone in their little ones' development. Only infrequently was Hephzibah able to go to Charleston; she found the trip quite an undertaking with an infant to tend to. Yet, she and Rachel thrived on the occasional opportunity to see each other face to face and admire their beautiful little ones.

News came that Rachel and her Captain Thomas were planning a move to Sumter, and Hephzibah regretted the distance that would separate them. Correspondence, she felt sure, would continue to prove a cathartic experience and a means of sharing her heart with a young mother with whom she had so much in common. The two had discovered that brides share many of the same problems and challenges. Maybe these were the lot of all newlyweds. Rachel discovered that her Thomas was very much a perfectionist, and Hephzibah owned that her Daniel was old enough to be decidedly set in his ways and crotchets.

She still corresponded with Eliza Pinckney, of course, but marriage and motherhood meant that they no longer had quite so much in common, what with Eliza still enjoying the role of belle in Charleston and Hephzibah a young matron. Sometimes Hephzibah felt that her own childhood was a lifetime away, and yet she would not change her station in life with anyone. She could not imagine life without Daniel and her little son. Maum Jean was still spry enough to give some attention to the baby's needs, and Hephzibah felt secure in knowing that her beloved nurse was keeping a watchful eye on little Daniel's growth and training. The painful reality, however, was that Maum Jean tired easily and often sat rocking the baby and crooning to him, her face alive with memories of rocking little ones through the years.

Maum Jean's great-niece, young Bella, helped out in the nursery in the evenings, but during the day she was frequently busy in the kitchen, learning some new trick with cooking and preserving. 'Rinthia visited her big sister Hephzibah nearly every week and each time she found a way to spend some time with Bella in the kitchen. They giggled, trying their hand at baking under the watchful eye of the Townsend's indulgent old cook and altogether just being little girls who were blissfully unconcerned about their widely different stations in life. They simply celebrated their mutual camaraderie.

In addition to her already full days, Hephzibah somehow managed to find time to direct the learning of the little ones in the plantation nursery. The law said that slaves could not be taught to read and write, but fortuitously, it was a law sometimes ignored. This was one of those matters that Hephzibah did not discuss with Daniel; she simply and quietly saw to it that Harriet, one of the young servants who was literate, spent some time in the nursery each week, teaching the children their letters and numbers. Harriet, one of the slaves who went with Hephzibah when she married, learned to read because Hephzibah had instructed the slave children on the Jenkins plantation. Little Miss Jenkins had only been ten herself when she started teaching a handful of the slave children. It was just another indication of the deeply engrained sense of justice that was so much a part of the character of Hephzibah Jenkins.

Here again, Daniel and his wife did not see eye to eye. He felt her too indulgent with the servants, but was forced to admit that to a person, they loved and respected his tiny dynamo of a wife. Very much in keeping with his time, Townsend simply did not view slavery as did Hephzibah, although he was never a cruel man. Hephzibah frequently felt Daniel was not understanding of his slaves, but she was thankful that at least he did not believe in harsh discipline. They might feel the edge of his tongue, but never the lash of a whip. He had their loyalty, but not the love that they, to a man, felt for Miz Hephzibah. Many times in the evening, she slipped down to the cabins with a bit of soothing broth for a sick servant, or an ointment to relieve the rash of a fretful baby. The unspoken blessing the Townsend slaves each sensed and cherished was the knowledge that they were viewed as a family and would not have to fear seeing their family torn apart. That happened too often for far too many, but not on the Townsend place. For this they thanked God. It somehow lessened the weight of their yoke.

The problem of a church was also a vexing one for the young wife. Of course, as a little girl Hephzibah had attended Edisto's Episcopal church with Papa and the family, but she far preferred the times they were in the Charleston house and she could visit First Baptist and hear Dr. Furman. Those Charleston trips were more difficult now, with a baby and additional responsibilities at home, but Sundays at First Baptist were always highlights for the devout young woman. Now that she was married, she usually, though with unspoken reluctance, attended services at the Presbyterian church with Daniel. His strong leadership in that congregation was evident, and he was widely respected for his calm good sense and business acumen. It was difficult for Hephzibah to explain, somehow, this gnawing sense of incompleteness she felt each time she worshipped. Her heart hungered for something deeper.

Each day in her personal time with God, Hephzibah would pour out her heart about doubts and misgivings, feelings both good and bad, but somehow needing an outlet whereby she might express her innermost thoughts and receive wise counsel. This was missing, and she longed for more understanding of the mysteries of life. Now she was a mother and increasingly aware of the responsibilities that would be hers for the spiritual wellbeing of their children. Often she yearned for Rachel to live nearby so they could exchange views and thoughts on the struggles that both of them were experiencing.

And even as the building of Bleak Hall progressed, so was the family growing. Late on the night of June 29, Hephzibah's second child was born and again it was a boy. Thomas Winborn Townsend announced his arrival into the world most vociferously; now young Daniel was a big brother. The birth had proceeded more smoothly than had her first, and Hephzibah was most thankful.

The increasingly busy young mistress was grateful for the invaluable help Maum Jean had provided by training a new Maum for the new young generation, and Jean's own great-niece Nancy was assuming this role with relish. Maum Nancy was young and lively and prone to wear a happy smile much of the time; she revealed a natural aptitude for nurturing little ones and was already devoted to young Daniel and baby Thomas. Maum Jean frequently just sat these days, rocking a little one and crooning her comforting Gullah songs that invariably could lull a baby to sleep.

For Hephzibah, some days just seemed to run together as she managed the plantation, cared for children, settled petty disputes among servants and soothed tears for a toddler who fell to rise and fall yet again. Every day usually ended in happy exhaustion. Daniel was more than busy with supervising crops, directing the skilled servants with construction of the new house and carrying on his leadership responsibilities at the church. Evenings in the parlor with Hephzibah were a chance for the two to catch up on the day, spend some special moments with the little ones, and talk over plans for furnishing the new plantation home.

One May evening in 1799, after Daniel and little Thomas, who was just taking his first steps, were tucked up in bed, Hephzibah and Daniel sat talking over their day. Hephzibah seemed quite big with news and for a moment, her words just seemed to hang in the air, then settle on Daniel's shoulder: She was expecting another baby. The rest of the day's news faded into insignificance, for Daniel was shocked to think of three children under three years old and Hephzibah not yet twenty herself. The difficulties this might mean for his young wife were a bit worrying to Townsend, but Hephzibah did not appear perturbed. Little Daniel looked to be a double for his fond father and baby Thomas had his mama's jet black hair, curls abounding. Now would they finally have a girl?

As the summer progressed, Hephzibah grew increasingly tired, but with such good help, she was able to get through the heat and humidity that hung over Edisto in late summer. Then in August, disaster struck. Malaria was ever the plague in the low country, and Edisto Island did not escape the pestilence. Babies seemed among the most vulnerable, and so it proved in the Townsend household. Several of the servants were bitten by the deadly mosquitoes, but all survived. Then baby Thomas began to run a fever, and as the days passed he grew increasingly lethargic. Hephzibah's tender heart grew more and more anguished. Day after day she soothed and bathed him, trying to reduce the fever, and forgetting all of her own discomfort and increasing awkwardness due to the new baby on the way. Through each night as little Thomas fretted and suffered, Hephzibah prayed for strength and courage, even as her heart seemed to fail within her.

~ *Eleven* ~

1799-1800

THOU THE REFUGE OF MY SOUL

Standing in the Jenkins burial ground, Daniel's arm supporting her, Hephzibah Townsend wept as Reverend McLeod prayed over their infant's grave. Thomas, her precious black-haired baby boy, not even fourteen months old, now gone forever. Tears made a path down the young mother's cheeks as sorrow threatened to overwhelm her. Ungainly with the weight of the new baby soon to come, Hephzibah allowed Daniel to gently lead her back to the carriage for the sad ride home. Surely this was a nightmare from which she would awake. Reality was all too stark; baby Thomas was now in the arms of Jesus. Only this thought comforted her grieving heart. She would see him once again in Glory.

All their work and effort on the new place, and now baby Thomas would never have a chance to grow up there. The question "why" came again and again to her anguished mind, but there was never an answer. Clinging to the comfort of talking with God and pouring out her heart to Him was her only solace. Daniel likewise was devastated, but a lifetime of bottling up his deepest emotions gave him an outward demeanor of calm. The only way he could express his sorrow was to hold Hephzibah close to his heart and somehow take part of her grief into himself.

Townsend poured himself into work on the new place. The

house was close to completion, and he was doubly eager now to finish the task. Moving into their own plantation home should serve as a good distraction for Hephzibah and help to occupy her sorrowing mind. Surely with everything that must be done and all the duties of each day, there was no time to spend sitting and grieving. That is, until night crept in upon them, and then the sorrow of loss flooded Hephzibah's mind afresh. She worked hard at not letting little Daniel see Mama cry. It tore at her for him to ask again and again, "But where is Brother? I want Brother." How could he possibly comprehend? Even she could not understand, much less explain to her two-year-old. Time and again, each day she would curve her hands around the new life growing in her and ask God to protect this little one and have mercy.

Daniel worked at keeping Hephzibah's mind busy in the evening planning for their move. If possible, he hoped to complete the house prior to the birth of the new baby. Earlier in the year they had made several trips to Charleston to purchase furnishings for Bleak Hall. Hephzibah planned to use some of her own favorite pieces from the Jenkins plantation and of course many items from their present house would make the move with them. With Bleak Hall being built on such a grand scale, however, much more was needed, and planning just what to purchase helped provide a diversion from dwelling on their ever-present grief.

September arrived, and the long-anticipated move into Bleak Hall began. Hephzibah's body was unwieldy by this time, and Townsend made sure her efforts were confined to directing the servants as to what to pack and exactly where it was to be placed in the large mansion soon to be their home. For her part,

Hephzibah made sure that Maum Jean merely supervised the servants in their tasks. Just watching her old nurse's slow steps and the stiffness of her bones as she stood up or sat down brought in upon Hephzibah the frailness of this one who had been a vital part of her entire life. Old Jack was even slower than Maum Jean, and their frailty was another tug on Hephzibah's tender heart. Little Bella seemed to sense her great-aunt's increasing weakness, and tended to spend more time in the nursery, fetching for Maum Jean and making her comfortable.

Late in the month the move was completed, or at least the Townsends were settled in enough to begin staying there. The move was exciting to young Daniel. He loved running from room to room, especially enjoying seeing his little rocking horse in its new home in the nursery. Little ones adjusted so quickly. Maum Jean watched the little fellow and smiled to herself, thinking of all the adjustments that had come in her long life, thinking back on all the places where she had lived. The new slave quarters had been finished for several weeks, but Maum Jean spent most of her time these days in the Bleak Hall nursery. Hephzibah joined her there a good portion of each day, feeling the weight of her advancing pregnancy and hoping this baby would soon be born.

Finally in October the baby decided to arrive. Another boy! John Ferrars Townsend made his entrance into the world with seemingly little effort. He delighted his parents with his fine lusty lungs and sturdy little frame. John seemed to thrive from the very first, and thankfully was a good baby who liked to sleep when it got dark. His hair promised to be the color of his proud father's, but his finely chiseled features had the look of Hephzibah about them, especially the shape of his eyes. Maum Nancy felt like this little one was hers, and Maum Jean smiled to see how the nursery had settled so quickly into a comfortable routine.

Being young and resilient, Hephzibah was soon as busy as ever, finding far more tasks to do each day than hours in which to do them. Baby John was placid and well-behaved, and Hephzibah loved the special moments she had in nursing him and singing the lullabies of her own childhood that were such a part of her. Occasionally, they made a trip to Charleston to gather new items for Bleak Hall, and life settled into a tranquil routine.

Then one night, Maum Jean came to Hephzibah with worry written across her lined face. Old Jack was having trouble breathing. Hephzibah made her way to their little cabin and sat down beside the man who had saved her life nearly twenty years before. His breathing was tortured, and it caused Hephzibah to catch her own breath and wish she could breathe for the weak old man. Quietly she sent a young servant to ride to Jenkins Plantation and tell Papa. He must know. Within the hour, Daniel Jenkins strode into the little cabin. One look at the dying man on the narrow bed was enough to tell the story. Jenkins knelt down beside the bed and took Jack's gnarled hand in his own. "Jack, Jack, can you hear me?" The old retainer opened his eyes at the voice of Massa Jenkins and a faint smile crossed his lined face. "Jack," Jenkins spoke again, "I want to tell you once again how much I thank you. I do thank you — you saved my baby's life. Jack, you did a brave and noble deed." Maum Jean was weeping as she soothed Jack's furrowed brow. And father and daughter both wept with her as life departed from the frail body of Jack and his soul entered eternity. There had never been a truer heart. And again, Hephzibah and Maum Jean made the trip to the family burial ground, their sorrow now compounded.

Maum Jean seemed to visibly shrink in the weeks that followed the loss of her husband. She could not even remember a time when Jack had not been in her life. For her part, Hephzibah had to steel herself to go through what she knew must be coming. That lined old face of her childhood Maum was as dear a part of her family as any soul could ever be, but now she was visibly fading before their very eyes.

Late one night, Maum Nancy quietly woke Hephzibah, whispering, "Aunty mighty low. You wanna come?" Quickly Hephzibah slipped into her flannel dressing gown, for the December wind was quite chilly at night. She hastened to Maum Jean's little cabin and in the flickering lantern light, could see her elderly nurse laboring to breathe. Hephzibah's heart was gripped with anguish as she knelt beside the bed, taking her dear nurse's hand into her own warm, young one.

"Maum Jean, are you hurting? What can we do to ease you?" but Maum Jean simply shook her head and whispered, "Ain't nothing, honey chile. I waiting for my time to glory." Hephzibah's strong young hand tightened briefly on that of her cherished Maum, as if there were some way she could pass some of her own strength on to one so dear.

"Miz Hephzibah, honey, you take keer of youself." The thready voice continued, " 'Thout old Jean here, you likes to do too much." Again she had to garner her strength to speak, "Jis' take keer of our babies, like I dun' take keer of you and you mama 'fore you," the frail woman finished in a whisper of a voice.

"Oh, Maum Jean, you are so dear to me; you are part of my life. You have always been here for me," Hephzibah's voice broke with anguish, "and I don't know why you have loved me so."

"Baby chile," Jean spoke again, "you always good to me. You always my honey chile." With labored breath she spoke again, "'You cain't help it, you jus' part of everything that dun stole my life." Stopping again to get her breath, she continued, "Miz Hephzibah, my body — it a slave, but my mind?" There was a long pause and then, "… it ain't. But you, chile, it's backards fo you." Maum Jean labored to finish her point, "You body, chile, it free. But you mind? Unh unh." Hephzibah was weeping as she heard the dying words of her cherished nurse, this one who knew her as well as did anybody on this earth. Maum Jean weakly reached up one frail finger and gently wiped away a tear, "Honey chile, I loved you fum de minute I brings you into this world. Now, chile, no more hurtin', no more pain."

Jean took one more labored breath, "Now my glory time." And with the words, a calm came across the furrowed brow and it was as if she could see beyond the night. As she departed her life of bondage, a brightness appeared to irradiate the dusky face of Hephzibah's beloved nurse, as if an unseen finger had smoothed those furrows away. Grief threatened to overtake her young Missus, and those profound words from the lips of a woman called a slave burned themselves into the fabric of Hephzibah's heart, never to depart; "You body, chile, it free. But you mind? Unh unh."

Once again Hephzibah stood in the Jenkins burial ground,

not far behind Cedar Grove Plantation. Hephzibah's childhood trips to spend time at Cedar Grove with Aunt Abby had been bright spots in those early years, but now there was grief in this place, as Hephzibah and Daniel sorrowfully laid Maum Jean to rest next to her beloved Jack. The hope of reunion in heaven was the assurance that comforted Hephzibah's bereft heart. During the brief words spoken at the grave, she relived in her mind her final night with Maum Jean. Those searing words, all spoken in love, would influence the remainder of her years.

The year 1799 had been a time of rejoicing: A healthy baby John had been born and the Townsends moved into their beautiful new plantation home. But it was even more a year of grieving, for Hephzibah had lost too many dear to her. First, baby Thomas, then her dear Jack, and now Maum Jean. Grief was a heavy load. It was an unseen burden, a weight heavier than an encumbrance that can be easily put aside. There was no place to lay down this burden of the soul. She did not tell Daniel about that dying conversation with Maum Jean, feeling it was a moment she needed to hold to herself. Hephzibah would never in all her life forget those last searching words from one who felt only love for her; those words had opened her mind to a hidden place she could not quite bring herself to examine.

For his part, Daniel could not understand the depth of grief Hephzibah felt over the loss of the two slaves who had been such an integral part of her life. He personally had never experienced such a thing, but he fretted over what it was doing to her. Townsend spoke few words of consolation, but showed an extra tenderness to her in small, unobtrusive ways, as if he himself wished to take on some of the weight of her sorrow.

In an effort to divert her mind, Daniel planned a Charleston trip, somehow sensing that a change of scenery and an opportunity for Hephzibah to visit her Baptist church there could work as a balm for her mourning heart. And it was good medicine. Christmas was fast approaching, and Hephzibah had an opportunity to talk quietly with Dr. Furman following the morning services. He spoke words of solace that brought a bit of resolution to her sense of loss. Focusing on the hope that is such a part of Christmas, the coming of peace into the world, helped Hephzibah deal with the pain of her losses.

Rachel Furman Baker had come home to Charleston from Sumter for the holidays, and the two young wives were able to spend a quiet day together talking over all the events of the past year. Their day together was like an early Christmas gift for Hephzibah, and watching the little boys playing and running together kept a smile on the faces of their mothers. There was a sense in which she could bare her soul to Rachel and know she would be understood; it was a catharsis that cut the edge of the heartache that had become her daily companion.

Townsend was relieved to be able to return to Edisto with a young wife whose deep-set dark eyes still sometimes appeared to be reflective pools of sorrow. But her sad moments were becoming less frequent and her natural zest for living seemed to be returning. Since childhood, Hephzibah had often displayed a quiet dignity, but sorrow had made it seem to nearly engulf her in too much quietness.

Now Townsend set into motion plans for celebrating their

first Christmas in the new place. An idea had come to him that might well cheer his young wife's heart during a period of discouragement, and he suggested that her brother move to Bleak Hall with them. Brother had graduated from Princeton and was learning skills as a planter. It proved to be the best of Christmas gifts. She and Brother had always shared a special bond, and having him as a part of their daily lives was a singular blessing. The babies adored him and his property was nearby; he could easily oversee his work from Bleak Hall. Just the thought of daily having Brother around put a new spring into Hephzibah's steps. Surely the Lord had important work ahead for her to do, and she needed to get busy with it. Yet even she, dreaming of how she might find her small point in this world, still had no idea of just how far-reaching God's plans for her would be.

Original icehouse, still standing on the site of Bleak Hall, Edisto Island. It stood close to the main house.

~ *Twelve* ~

1800-1802
New Beginnings

A new century! New Year's celebrations on Edisto seemed especially joyful this time around, bringing in not just the hope of a new year but a brand new start in a dynamic new nation. The new year also brought additional tidings of a personal nature to Hephzibah. She was expecting yet again. Surely not this soon. But it was a fact; she knew the telltale signs all too well. Daniel's response this time was just to lift his eyebrows, cock his head to one side and suggest, "Another boy, you think?!" This time however, the pregnancy seemed especially difficult. Hephzibah was keenly aware of the absence of her beloved Maum, always there before to encourage and soothe. Maum Jean had instinctively known how to calm her heart, but this time Hephzibah must garner courage on her own. Maum Jean had trained Nancy in midwife skills for several years, but it would not be quite the same. Thankfully, Aunt Abby was not too far away. She had only had one child herself, but she had grandchildren now and was ever a practical and no-nonsense kind of aunt. Aunt Abby always had a way of giving you advice that didn't feel like advice. A person simply felt it was her own idea all along. Hephzibah became more and more dependent on Abby's bracing kind of encouragement, for this was a difficult pregnancy.

Come June of that first year of the new century, Hephzibah lost her baby. Tiny Isaac came far too early, only six months along; he never drew a breath. The Townsends felt the grief of loss and a sense of wondering what might have been, all over again. Nonetheless, Hephzibah's spirit quickly rebounded, and she resumed her usual busy schedule within just a few days. By the end of the year, she knew she was to have another child the following spring or early summer. Little Daniel and baby John were both flourishing, and life took on a steady tenor.

The even keel of life did not last long. The winter of 1800 was harsh for the low country, and Hephzibah's father grew ill. Within a matter of weeks, Daniel Jenkins's condition was most disturbing. The doctor began coming to check on him frequently, and Hephzibah found this alarming; Papa had always seemed so strong, almost indestructible. He was only fifty years old, and in the prime of life. In late January, when several days had elapsed since visiting him, Hephzibah was shocked to note his sunken eyes and pale skin. Dr. Hopkinson had delivered a diagnosis just that morning: pneumonia.

The weeks passed with no sign of improvement. In spite of the doctor's best efforts, Jenkins's condition grew steadily worse and it soon became apparent that he was seriously ill. Hephzibah went daily to spend time at his bedside, still in disbelief that her strong and steady Papa was growing weaker by the moment. Some afternoons, Brother could go with her, and together they sat at his bedside.

One early February afternoon, with only Jenkins, his wife, and Hephzibah in the room, he appeared to become acutely aware of the fragility of his wife. Martha had never been resolute in nature, and she was visibly anguished at his worsening condition in spite of the fact that all of them had worked to shield her from worry as best they could. Only after Martha had left the room that winter evening, nervously wringing her hands as she walked out the door with downcast head, did Jenkins take Hephzibah by the hand and appeal to her, "Daughter, you are the strong one." Jenkins paused and painfully coughed. "If I don't pull through, please help Martha with the children. She will not know where to turn, you know."

Hephzibah's heart contracted with pain at the very thought of losing her father. "Papa, you are young, you are strong. You must fight — Papa, you will make it, surely," she spoke as if her very words could convince the both of them.

Slowly and deliberately shaking his head, Jenkins continued, "Daughter, you must promise me." Hephzibah fervently assured him, but pled again, "Papa, just rest; garner your strength. All of us need you."

Jenkins patted her hand and spoke haltingly, but with fierce determination: "Hephzibah, there is already far too much on you for one so young. But then, I have always known, even when you were a little girl, that you were an old soul." He hesitated, then gave his lopsided little smile, "Somehow God gifted you with wisdom beyond your years." Jenkins stopped, then picked up his thoughts again, "Child, I want you to have the silver coffee pot and set. Each time you use it, remember your papa was always so proud of his daughter." Hephzibah's eyes brimmed over by this time, and a tear dropped on the trembling hand holding hers.

"I made out a will, my dear," Jenkins spoke again, "I want all the servants that are kin to those who went with you when you married to go to Bleak Hall with you." Daniel had difficulty speaking now. "I'm worried about our faithful servants, Daughter. I can trust you to keep an eye out for their welfare. You know, Child, that Martha won't know how to cope."

Jenkins seemed to need reassurance from his strong daughter; their bond had always been so close. "Watch out for your brothers and sisters, Hephzibah. You'll be a comfort to Martha. She means well; she just isn't strong." Her heart wringing with anguish, Hephzibah hastened to lay her father's heart at rest. He could not doubt that the welfare of each one, servant and family alike, was just as deeply the concern of his daughter as well. Returning to Bleak Hall that cold winter evening, Hephzibah felt far older than her years, dreading what appeared to fast be coming.

Within days, Jenkins no longer had the strength to talk, and Hephzibah and Brother sat at his side much of those final days, helplessly watching the life and vitality drain out of his body. Daniel Jenkins, planter, justice of the peace, senator, Episcopal vestryman and loving father, died February 1801, only fifty years old.

In addition to their own abject grief, Hephzibah and her brother had the sorrowful task of comforting both their stepmother and six bereft young siblings, all struggling to make sense of their world that had just turned upside down. Poor Martha was prone to sit and weep and wring her hands. It fell to Hephzibah and Brother to get a grip on their own tearing sorrow and try to instill some sense of courage and acceptance into their distraught stepmother. Their most successful tactic seemed to be to help her focus on how much her children, especially the little ones, depended on her and how desperately they needed Mama to be their security. It was necessary for Hephzibah and her brother to make all the arrangements, and Daniel Townsend laid aside all but his most pressing responsibilities in order to be a bulwark to Hephzibah in this fresh sorrow. And to her, the knowledge of her glad reunion in heaven with Papa one day was balm to her grieving heart.

Two active little boys, a large plantation home with many servants to direct, and a rapidly advancing pregnancy proved good therapy for the resilient Hephzibah Jenkins Townsend, who had not yet reached her twentieth birthday. Hephzibah was delighted with Daniel's idea for their icehouse. It would be a necessity come summer, and his suggestions for its design drew a delighted response from her. Townsend had the workmen construct an icehouse shaped like a tiny private chapel, complete with mock tracery windows and a gable roof with its triangular dormers. Chapel-style windows were a finishing touch. The little icehouse, finished in gleaming white paint, brought a sense of calm to Hephzibah's heart, just looking at it. Townsend had found a special way to comfort his young wife's heart.

Papa's will, adding to the number of slaves who came to Hephzibah, was still a further responsibility, forcing Hephzibah yet again to consider her personal burden of owning slaves. And it was a burden. There was no other word for it. Nearly all the plantation families of Edisto, indeed of the low country, seemed to think this was just "things as they are," but Hephzibah continued to find it disturbing. And only this past year, with the coming of a new century, had come a new law prohibiting the importing of additional slaves, thus making those presently in the country just that much more valuable. Already, some 90 percent of Edisto's population was black. This circumstance did nothing to ease the dichotomy in Hephzibah's heart. Things were "this way," but how could they be right?

She read her Scripture faithfully and was beginning to get tired of hearing people say, "Well, there's slavery in the Bible." Those slaves in Bible times had been slaves in far different circumstances; that world had been vastly different. And how could you read the new U.S. Constitution and note that all people are created equal, but then realize it wasn't really so at all? Theory and reality did not match. Yet inevitably, her thoughts returned to a question: *And what can a woman do?* Nothing. That seemed the logical answer. *But surely,* her thoughts raced on, *there is something I can do.* And, not for the first time, she reflected: *I do suspect that God plants yearnings in us so that we will at least try to change the course of things.* Hephzibah felt quite alone in her feelings, however. She could not name a friend on Edisto who seemed to share her sentiments on owning another person. That did nothing to deter her uncomfortable thoughts, and the burning words of Maum Jean the night she died rang in the young mother's ears at the most surprising moments.

There was precious little time to sit around thinking deep thoughts, however, with all that must be done. In addition to an already full schedule, there were the added needs of her stepmother. Martha was awash in grief and turned to Hephzibah for advice nearly every day. 'Rinthia was already spending much of her time at Bleak Hall, and young Martha, now an active nine-year-old, came with her on many days. They always wanted to spend time with the young slave Bella. Since Bella worked in the kitchen, that spot often seemed full of young girls and fragrant scents. The older boys — Ben, Thomas and Richard — were all studying with their tutor, and Martha was mainly occupied with caring for four-year-old Joseph and trying to handle all the affairs of the plantation. She constantly asked Hephzibah for advice, and her stepdaughter was most thankful that Brother was helping out with practical matters around the Jenkins place. Townsend himself often stood ready with advice when Brother turned to him to call on his vast experience in running a large plantation.

The last week of May 1801, Hephzibah again gave birth. To no one's surprise, it was a boy. He was given a special family name: Jonathan Frampton. It seemed fitting, for Hephzibah's grand-father Jonathan had inherited the valuable tract of land from his father, John Frampton. The original land had cost a princely twelve thousand pounds and had passed from Jonathan to his granddaughter. A tired Hephzibah remarked that May evening to Daniel that he may have gotten a late start on becoming a father but had certainly made up for lost time. Her husband smiled in agreement and remarked, "My very dear, to think, you have given birth to five sons, and you're just now twenty-one years old!"

Hephzibah had been too swamped with constant tasks and another new baby on the way at any moment to note the passing of such a milestone birthday, but Townsend had not forgotten. Knowing her penchant for lovely teapots, he gave her for her birthday an exquisite three-tiered Chinese teapot in a delicate willow pattern. It became an evening ritual to have her special blend of pekoe tea from her blue-and-white porcelain teapot.

Tiny Jonathan was smaller than his brother John had been, but had a head full of hair as black and shiny as his young mother's. Those round baby eyes, however, were as crystal blue as Daniel Townsend's own. For his part, Brother delighted in the three boys and bragged on his nephews to anyone who would listen. Hephzibah secretly wished that Brother would find that right young woman, fall in love and have lovely children of his own. He would make a wonderful father. Daniel Jenkins, however, did not seem in any hurry, so Hephzibah kept her thoughts pretty well to herself, although she kept her eyes open for likely candidates among her friends on neighboring plantations. There were two cousins of theirs, Phoebe and Ann, both of whom were winsome young women, but Brother did not show any particular interest in either his cousins or the other young Edisto girls who thought him most eligible. Maybe he wanted to wait until he was older to marry, like Townsend had done.

In the months to follow the loss of her papa, Hephzibah frequently reflected on how hungry her soul felt for more spiritual nourishment. Trips to Charleston were only scattered, but those Sundays of worship on Church Street always brought a sense of renewal to her spirit. She could usually find a few minutes to talk with Dr. Furman and always had a question or two stored up to ask him at those times.

Knowing that a century earlier there had been a little Baptist congregation on Edisto caused her to have the recurring thought that surely there could be one again. In fact, William Screven, that marvelous Baptist pioneer who had founded the Charleston church well over a century earlier, had been the one who began Baptist work on Edisto. Hephzibah had learned from Papa that her ever-so-great-aunt, Providence Grimball, had been baptized by Dr. Screven. Once and again, Hephzibah would contemplate how special it would be to have a Baptist church right here near home. The thought was never far away. And periodically, following a particularly moving sermon, she would mention to Dr. Furman that it would be wonderful if just occasionally he could come to Edisto and hold a service there. Furman did not laugh the idea away, but would usually respond that it was something he would certainly consider. The possibility gave Hephzibah hope, and thoughts of such an eventuality slowly but surely took firm hold in her mind.

Another new year, 1802, and with it the realization that yet again she was expecting. Hephzibah smiled to herself just thinking about giving the news to Daniel. His immediate reaction would likely be to guess that it was bound to be another boy. Hephzibah herself was also resigned to giving birth just to male children and shook her head to think of having six children by the age of twenty-one. If idle hands were the devil's workshop, he was certainly out of luck around Bleak Hall. Hephzibah began the new year with a fervent wish that 1802 would not be a repeat of the previous one, but instead a year of hope and promise, with the sorrows of death behind them.

Avenue of live oaks leading to Botany Bay Plantation, location of Bleak Hall on Edisto Island, South Carolina.

— *Thirteen* —

1802-1803

BLEAK HALL

Turning that curve down the road lined with live oaks and coming upon the sight of Bleak Hall always caused Hephzibah to catch her breath and feel a fresh sense of awe at the beauty of home. She loved hearing the crunch of carriage wheels on the crushed oyster-shell drive and looking up to see the magnificent façade of their new plantation home. Its crowning touch was the gleaming white hexagonal cupola that crowned the three-story edifice. There was nothing commonplace about Bleak Hall, from its myriad windows shining when the bright sun fell on them to the inviting depth of the porch that girdled the front.

To top it all, the mighty Atlantic Ocean flowed just a mere mile away, its waves washing up from distant shores and making themselves at home on nearby Botany Bay Island. Hephzibah oft times wondered what this land must have looked like to the Indians who had lived and hunted these thick, primeval woods just a few hundred years earlier. As a little girl, she thrilled to hear the stories Papa told them about the smugglers and pirates who landed right along this little section of the Atlantic coast. Returning from any daily errand invariably brought Hephzibah a serene sense of being back home, this place that was now such a part of her.

The halls and parlors were redolent with beeswax and lemon oil, kept sparkling and fresh by the small army of servants who lovingly cared for each room. The appreciative smile on Miz Hephzibah's face as she noticed the extra care they lent to their work always spurred them to even greater efforts. Each gleaming surface was bright enough to use for a mirror, especially the shining length of the magnificent mahogany banquet table.

Hephzibah loved seeing the little treasures of vases, delicate pitchers, and a myriad of knick-knacks from various eras of family history, each in its place. Every one of them told a story, and Hephzibah was already telling her little ones and 'Rinthia and Martha about these treasures and about the ancestors who collected and cared for each cherished piece. It was never too early to teach a child to show respect for those who had come before them.

She enjoyed taking her sons by the hand and looking at the massive shelves of books lining the walls of the new library and telling young Daniel and three-year-old John that these books "hold treasures, too, and someday you will discover these treasures for yourselves." Daniel was a sturdy five-year-old by now and eagerly learned his alphabet. He could already read several of the children's books his fond father kept purchasing. Hephzibah especially enjoyed reminding the children of the story of the silver tankard, her treasured gift from Papa. She told them of those special times in her childhood when Papa would use the silver container and repeat the tale of how he had ordered it all the way from England. For a special treat, she would occasionally pour a tiny bit of coffee from the tankard and mix it with a generous portion of milk and sugar so each child could have a bit of "morning coffee."

It was February of 1802 and Hephzibah was thinking ahead to summer and the birth of baby number six. Thank God at least three were still living. Infant mortality was not at all uncommon, but that did not keep it from being a blow to her heart. She would be twenty-two in May, but some days she felt like an old woman. Be that as it may, no one seeing those shining curls and sparkling eyes could picture Hephzibah as anything other than a radiant young bride. A closer look into her deep, dark eyes, however, revealed a glimpse of unspoken pain, unexpressed but nonetheless real. There had been more than enough sorrow in the past three years.

'Rinthia was already twelve and spending much of her time at Bleak Hall, learning many skills from her older sister and becoming entrenched as a prime favorite with her little nephews. Martha was not far behind, and although only ten, bid fair to equal her big sister in charm and aptitude. She was also picking up handy skills in the kitchen, as she and 'Rinthia spent countless hours there with Bella and Cook.

Cook was feeling her age, with joints that protested at standing for long hours. She found good use for the eager young hands that helped with mixing, kneading, fetching ingredients from the spacious pantry and sampling her special cookies. The girls also spent a good bit of time studying with the new tutor hired to teach young Daniel. For her part, Bella was the keenest student in the plantation nursery class. Hephzibah paid particular attention to her progress. Bella was like a living link to her beloved Maum

Jean. God being her helper, Hephzibah was going to do right by this precious child.

Hephzibah's weekly visit with her stepmother on the Jenkins plantation in early February was upsetting. Martha looked drawn and peaked and was coughing with frightening regularity. "Have you seen the doctor, Mama?" was Hephzibah's immediate question. Of course Martha had not sent word to him. Hephzibah did so at once and stayed until Dr. Hopkinson was able to come and check on her stepmother. After examining Martha, he called Hephzibah aside and shaking his head, told her to prepare herself. Mrs. Jenkins had dangerously advanced consumption. Hephzibah's heart sank, not only with pity for the diffident Martha, but for the impact of what this would mean for all of her half brothers and sisters.

After calling in the servants to acquaint them with the gravity of the problem and instructing them as to how to care for their mistress, she immediately sent word to Uncle Micah and also to Aunt Elizabeth, who had married Paul Fripp. Both of these siblings of Papa's had been helpful and supportive of Martha since their brother Daniel had died, and now they could be a real comfort to her. Furthermore, Hephzibah needed their advice.

'Rinthia and Martha began remaining at Bleak Hall so as not to be exposed to possible infection. The boys — Benjamin, Thomas and Richard — were busy each day with their tutor. At sixteen, Benjamin was close to being ready for Princeton. The youngest, five-year-old Joseph, was going to need care, and Aunt Elizabeth came to the rescue, taking her little great nephew to their nearby plantation. Martha was rapidly weakening now and Hephzibah spent much of her time at Jenkins Plantation, directing the work of the house and seeing to Martha's every comfort. Although Hephzibah was expecting again, it was still early days and she managed to run two plantations with practiced skill. Daniel was being a tremendous help, and Brother managed to come spend time with his stepmother several times a week.

Come the end of March, Martha's frail body failed. Hephzibah and Brother knew the signs all too well. Their frail stepmother seemed to have no will to fight the disease that ravaged her body. Martha Jenkins died quietly in her sleep that last day of March, and it fell to Hephzibah to tell the children. The older boys were in a state of shock; the world as they knew it was now no more. 'Rinthia and Martha clung to their big sister and drew strength from her. Hephzibah and Daniel quickly decided that the girls needed to live with them. Young Joseph could not understand what had happened in his life and depended on his Aunt Elizabeth to right his world again.

Again came the sad procession to the Jenkins burial ground. This was growing far too familiar to Hephzibah, and some mornings she awoke thinking what else might possibly happen in their ordered world that was no longer ordered.

Brother was able to speed young Benjamin's matriculation to Princeton, and a whole new phase of life started for this half brother. Uncle Micah and Aunt Margaret took Thomas and Richard home with them, and the boys' tutor continued to guide them in their studies. They sorely needed a sense of normalcy about their lives now shattered by the loss of both parents within one brief year. Little Joseph had settled in with Aunt Elizabeth, but Hephzibah saw to it that each week he was able to spend some time with his sisters at Bleak Hall.

Spring was in riotous bloom again, just as though nothing untoward had occurred. Would life ever be normal again? Whatever normal was. Hephzibah had forgotten. Daniel was her stronghold, and she relied on his rock-solid dependability. The bond between the two seemed to strengthen in the face of adversity. Daniel and Brother were assuming primary responsibility for seeing that the stipulations of Papa's will were followed. It was a massive job to decide what to do about the land and holdings until the children were old enough to control their inheritance.

According to Jenkins's wishes, Jane, that marvel in the kitchen, was to come to Brother upon the death of Martha. This proved to be a boon to all of them, for Cook was quite old and more than happy to retire to her snug little cabin and have someone wait on her for a change. Jane stepped into the role of head cook, and Bella was thrilled. For her part, Jane poured her knowledge and skills into the brilliant young slave who showed such an aptitude for cooking. Jane was not quite as indulgent with 'Rinthia and Martha but did allow them a certain amount of leeway; Jane revealed a soft spot in her introspective heart for the two Jenkins girls who treated her with respect. Jane had always sensed the affection and respect accorded her by Maum Jean's favorite, Miz Hephzibah, and she had quickly acclimated herself to life at Bleak Hall.

In later life, Hephzibah looked back on that period in her life and reflected on how tragedy had seemed to dog their steps. Martha Seabrook Jenkins had not been long in her resting place at the burial grounds when their sturdy Daniel, five years old, fell sick. Young Daniel had had very few childhood diseases and was as bright and quick as ever a child that walked, but somehow, in May of this year, 1802, he fell quite ill. Dr. Hopkinson was puzzled at first, but as young Daniel worsened, a telltale rash began to erupt and the doctor sadly made the diagnosis of scarlet fever.

Terror gripped Hephzibah, for this child had always been so strong and bright. Scarlet fever was contagious, so the other children were not allowed in his room. Regardless of contagion, Hephzibah and Daniel spent much of their days at his beside. Fever raged, and he would cry out that his head was hurting and plead with Mama to stop the pain. Helplessly they watched their firstborn fail a little each day. And during the endless night of June 13, as Hephzibah and Daniel knelt helplessly beside his little bed, Daniel Townsend IV quietly died. A little piece of his mother's heart died in that moment, and she and Daniel clung to each another in helpless anguish.

Hephzibah walked blindly to the garden late that night, tracing a path endlessly back and forth, trying to siphon off her grief. *Oh God, oh God, why? Why?* There was no answer to be heard on the still night air. That inner force of character, such an essential part of Hephzibah Townsend, reasserted itself — and she did what she had to do, comforting young John Ferrars, who simply couldn't understand what death meant. Why was Big Brother in heaven? He wanted him here. Jonathan was just a year old now, and could not grasp the loss. There was a new and silent grief hovering about Daniel, and Hephzibah could read it in the lines of his face. She tried to spend as much time as possible with him. The evenings were the hardest; they would sit in the parlor after family devotion time and each evening, sorrow would rush in on each of them all over again. Little Daniel's spot was empty.

But there was new life to come, and Hephzibah worked hard at not questioning the Almighty. She comforted herself with the thought she would be with her beloved firstborn forever in heaven. There was this new empty spot in her heart however, and she was thankful for more to do in the day than there was time to do it. And then the new baby made its appearance, arriving early in the morning hours of August 14. This time Hephzibah did not even think to ask, "Boy or girl?" — as if it were already a foregone conclusion. Sure enough, they named their newest son Richard Moncrief, this little fellow with his surprisingly light hair combined with deep, dark eyes and healthy lungs. John Ferrars was charmed with his new sibling, and Hephzibah welcomed the latest distraction. 'Rinthia, Martha and Bella all vied with each other for time with the beautiful new baby, and he proved good therapy for all of them.

However, death wasn't through with them yet. Baby Richard was only a month old when Jonathan, just fifteen months old himself, came down with croup and struggled mightily to breathe. Dr. Hopkinson fought alongside them for the life of this child, but it was not to be, and in September Jonathan lost his fight. Hephzibah's eyes blurred over with tears as she and Daniel stood in that far-too-familiar place in the Jenkins burial ground and saw this precious son laid next to his brothers. And somehow her broken heart managed to bring the words to her anguished spirit, "The Lord giveth and the Lord taketh away. Blessed be the name of the Lord." Then a fervent prayer would work its way into that grieving heart: "Oh God, please no more. Just give me strength and grace for the day. That's all I ask. Keep us safe 'til the storm passes by." Little though Hephzibah realized it during those dark days, God had special plans for her life in the years to come.

Fourteen

1803-1804
FROM EVERY SWELLING TIDE OF WOE

Bleak Hall was a massive place with room aplenty for a large family, but when 1803 rolled around, only two of the Townsend's six sons had survived to greet the new year there. 'Rinthia and Martha Jenkins were part of the family now, and their little brother Joseph stayed with them part of most weeks. What with supervising her younger siblings along with her own children, Hephzibah never had to worry about being bored. She just wished for more time.

On most Sundays she would attend services at the Presbyterian church with Daniel, but just occasionally Hephzibah could get to Charleston for a weekend and worship at First Baptist and hear Dr. Furman preach. 'Rinthia was thirteen now and usually went with her. The young teenager was excellent help with John and baby Richard when Hephzibah took them along. Occasionally, Rachel would be back from Sumter visiting her family in Charleston, and just a few hours with her longtime friend gave Hephzibah's heart a much-needed lift. Those Sundays in Charleston were balm to her lacerated emotions. The past two years had taken its toll, and her soul desperately sought spiritual solace.

Life seemed to take on an even keel by the time summer arrived. Brother was busy with his plantations, and Daniel always had more to do than hours in the day. He and Hephzibah had learned a bit about compromise in these some eight years of marriage, but her ever-present force of character, which he had so admired in the young girl he courted, was an increasing irritation to him now. At forty-four, Townsend was growing increasingly inflexible. At the same time, it went against the grain for Hephzibah to have to turn to him for permission to make certain purchases, and to have to ask Daniel's opinion on matters that she considered her purview. Knowing that so much of their funds — as well as the majority of their land — came from her inheritance made it just that much more galling, never mind what the law said. Sometimes she nearly ground her teeth in frustration.

A good outlet for her angst, however, was to spend some time with Aunt Abby and glean from Aunt's years of experience something about the art of compromise. Abby had learned to practice accommodation in both her first marriage to Joseph Murray and later when she married Ephraim Mikell, and she passed on bits and pieces of wisdom to her young relative in such a way that they were palatable to the headstrong young wife.

Hephzibah's deeply ingrained sense of justice was another sore point for her husband, who did not view fairness through the same lenses. Townsend took for granted his male prerogative in making unilateral decisions and found it annoying when Hephzibah did not automatically acquiesce to his more-seasoned judgment. They certainly didn't view slavery through the same filter.

After a time of especially acrimonious disagreements, Hephzibah usually found that a visit to Aunt Abby was helpful in calming her down. The older woman's sage advice helped her devise ways to subtly maneuver through the sometimes boisterous shoals of domestic disharmony, as she liked to call it. Papa's indulgent style of fatherhood had allowed free rein to Hephzibah's natural bent toward decisiveness. Jenkins had relied on her judgment even when she was quite small, allowing her to take on more responsibility than did most young heiresses. This had proved a factor in the difficult transition to her role as a wife, and there were frequent bumps in the road to domestic tranquility.

Nonetheless, the Townsends were usually able to come to some sort of understanding, even after a particularly volatile disagreement. Neither enjoyed giving ground to the other, and it made for some lively discussions. Sometimes the angry heat staining Hephzibah's cheeks revealed the depth of her temper, and she would bite her tongue to keep from making things worse. A young woman with her "force of character" did not enjoy being forced into a decision not of her own choosing. But on the other hand, Hephzibah would occasionally just stop, take a deep breath and give her beguiling smile. It nearly always had the power to move Daniel to hold his tongue and even occasionally to concede a point.

However, there was not a great deal of time to waste on domestic discord when there was so much that needed doing. The plantation was flourishing, and Bleak Hall was producing quality Sea Island Cotton that was gaining a stellar reputation on the European market. But in the summer of 1803, malaria was a severe problem, and in August little Richard contracted the fever. Within days he was desperately ill; despite all their efforts to get the fever down, their precious toddler died the week following his first birthday, and Hephzibah's agony returned. Their first son had been born in 1797 and now, six years later, five small graves lay next to each other in the Jenkins burial ground. Hephzibah could scarcely come to grips with the magnitude of all the loss. Once again, she and Daniel tried to comfort each another, and young John wandered around looking solemn-eyed and lonely. Each one was desperately trying to understand all the sorrow that dogged their footsteps.

Within weeks of losing her baby, Hephzibah realized she was expecting another child. It felt like the grief was imploding on her. Here was another little life coming, but would this be like nearly all the others, one to love and then lose so tragically? Often in the long night hours, she would lie awake in the still and sultry summer air, eyes wide open, asking the silent question yet again, "Why, God? Why?"

Thank goodness for duties. Thank God for endless tasks. Being busy always helped, and a bumper cotton crop that year was encouraging to the Townsends and also to Brother, who was busy with the crops on nearby Shargould Plantation and his other properties as well. Hephzibah's half brothers and sisters were coming to grips with their loss, and Benjamin wrote cheering letters of his first months at Princeton. Her other brothers, Thomas and Richard, were studying hard with their tutor and hoping to join Ben in New Jersey within the next couple of years.

Spring of 1804 arrived, and spring always brought a new sense of hope. Hephzibah's pregnancy had been quite smooth this time, and she worked hard at not daydreaming about this baby possibly being a girl. It hadn't happened in the past eight years, so she didn't allow herself much time to dwell on thoughts of a daughter.

Brother had just bought a new boat this spring and was anxious to give it a good try, so he and their two half brothers planned to take it for a maiden voyage, making the short trip to Beaufort. The morning of March 14 dawned chilly but bright and clear — not a cloud in the sky. Cousins Henry and John Bailey, Benjamin Scott from St. Helena Island, and their friend Mr. Wood from Beaufort went on board with Daniel Jenkins and his younger brothers Richard and Thomas. Jenkins was taking twelve of his strong young servants along, and they were doing the work of rowing. As they set sail from Frampton's Inlet on Jenkins's property, all were anticipating a speedy and carefree trip to Beaufort. Hephzibah watched the vessel leave the wharf, she and other relatives waving from the shore and wishing them bon voyage.

Just minutes after Hephzibah had turned and headed home, the shining new vessel struck a bank and the vessel capsized in the water. At that very time, there were slaves working along the shore in nearby Edingsville who heard the cries of the oarsmen and quickly sent for help. A crowd gathered within minutes, but just as several men were setting out to rescue the young sailors, a sudden squall blew up. The sea, which moments before had been smooth as glass, was now a raging turmoil of roiling waves under a suddenly darkened sky. By this time the capricious heavens had formed a deep gray mist that clung to the surface of the water. It was impossible to see through its thick mass. Each attempt to launch a rescue boat on the rolling waves ended in failure, and those on the shore could only stand by helplessly and pray.

Then with the same suddenness with which it had appeared, the storm was gone, and the sea like glass yet again. A murmur went through the waiting crowd on the shore as they could finally make out the image of a dark object in the distance. As it drew nearer, eyes could make out the figure of a man clinging to a piece of wreckage. It was Cousin Henry Bailey. He alone of all those on board Daniel Jenkins's new boat survived.

Someone sped in the direction of Bleak Hall to alert Hephzibah to what was happening, and she rushed back to a scene of unbelievable loss. Brother? Gone? It could not be; this one who was so much a part of all her life, now forever gone? The magnitude of the tragedy was too large to even wrap her mind around. A devastated Hephzibah Townsend, nearly nine months pregnant and already made vulnerable by far too much loss, could not imagine losing Brother, Thomas and Richard, all within a day. No. Surely not.

It was night before the bodies washed up on shore and were recovered, but Hephzibah felt her soul could never rebound. And Daniel Townsend, who had truly loved Daniel Jenkins like his own brother, valiantly strove to move beyond his own wrenching grief to comfort Hephzibah. Was there any comfort for such stunning loss? Hephzibah clung to Daniel and kept crying over and over, "Tell me it isn't true. Tell me it isn't true. Surely it didn't happen." Townsend simply wept with her and held her close.

Although Hephzibah Townsend lived a long and full life, the sense of loss experienced that dreadful day never quite went away. Brother had always been part of Hephzibah's life; the bond between them a beautiful thing to see. It was like losing part of herself. The *Charleston Courier* held the story of the disaster in its paper of March 16, and all of Edisto Island was in mourning at the magnitude of their tragedy.

In later years, Hephzibah had no clear recollection of what went on during those terrible days, the recovery of the bodies, the funerals, the services at the newly dug graves. The Jenkins burial ground now held more of her immediate family than did Bleak Hall. It just could not be true, yet she knew it was. Ever after, Hephzibah Townsend looked on those days as the dark night of the soul. Literally heavy with child, for her baby was due any moment, she was nonetheless too restless to sit still for long. Several evenings she got away from everyone and headed down to the nearby salt marshes, walking, crying, praying. Vainly she struggled to accept the scope of the tragedy. Thomas and Richard — gone beyond all recovery? Never again to sit and talk and laugh and share her deepest thoughts and hopes with Brother? Oh, God. Sometimes she just wanted to tuck the darkness around her grieving heart and somehow not see reality. It was far too painful. The only thought that eased her aching heart was the knowledge that they would all one day be together in heaven with the Lord.

Hephzibah had the sense of being a stone caught up in an avalanche as it rolled downhill, as events had overtaken her and moved her along without her connivance or permission. Some nights she would lie in bed, her hands on her swollen abdomen and eyes wide open, silently petitioning God, pleading with Him to wake up from His slumber and hear her cries. "God, oh God, all this heartache. Where are you?" Again, and yet again, she would strive to touch all that aching sadness, and the silent tears would simply trickle down her cheeks, for the words to pray were absolutely beyond her. She helplessly repeated again and again the two words that expressed the depths of her agony, "Oh God, oh God, oh God," like a litany voiced to the gates of heaven itself. Slowly, slowly she began to sift through the shattered pieces of her life, to see what could be salvaged to help her face the days ahead.

Daniel swallowed his own grief and did all that was necessary with arrangements, services, and legal duties to perform. Hephzibah broke down yet again when Townsend gently told her that Brother had left Shargould and all his property to her, to use as she best saw fit.

Five-year-old John Ferrars could not begin to comprehend all that had happened. Two sad young aunts spent a lot of time with the little boy, trying to help him cope with the sorrow engulfing Bleak Hall. He especially liked to go to the kitchen where Bella always had a special treat for him, and Jane, too, indulged the little fellow who had a special place in her heart. Thankfully, John had begun lessons with a tutor, and this helped keep him occupied and not dwelling on the sorrow that hung over the plantation.

Hephzibah felt like time had stopped, but grief itself did not slow down. It had become her constant companion. Yet in the midst of the depths of sorrow, nature took over and Hephzibah went into labor. She nearly welcomed the pain, because her heart was hurting so deeply that it seemed the pangs of child-birth would feel right at home. In the early evening of March 24, ten days after the massive tragedy, a little miracle came into the world. Hephzibah could scarcely believe her eyes when she saw her newborn for the first time. A girl! For the first time in what seemed a lifetime of sorrow, a smile broke across the young mother's face and those deep-set eyes glowed with incandescent light. So certain had she and Townsend been that this baby would be another boy that they had not even picked out a girl's name.

A tired but grateful Hephzibah held her daughter, all sweetly powdered and wrapped in her little blanket, and made her acquaintance. In wonder all over again, she counted each little finger and every little toe. Perfect. The tiny face was framed with jet black hair, an amazing amount of it. Baby opened her eyes, and unfocused though they were, they seemed to gaze back with the same deep, rich color of her mother's. "Mary," breathed Hephzibah, "this is Mary." She smiled, "Mary, you're our very first daughter. A girl! You will be Mary Frampton!" A grinning Daniel Townsend gently took his tiny daughter into his arms, his eyes beaming with pride. Maum Nancy slipped into the room with 'Rinthia and Martha, young John Ferrars right on their heels. He was enthralled with his little sister. Mama even let him carefully hold her for a few moments and he nearly burst with pride.

When late that night of March 24, 1804, Hephzibah finally closed her weary eyes, she drifted off to sleep on a prayer of thanksgiving to God. It was as if He had sent her a special gift, and this gift seemed like the promise of His presence. Her thoughts wrapped around the passage from Psalms that had so often given her hope: "Weeping may endure for the night. But joy cometh in the morning." Tiny Mary Frampton Townsend was a cherished harbinger of hope.

— *Fifteen* —

1804-1807
'TIL THE STORM PASSES BY

Hephzibah could swear that by the time Mary Frampton was two months old, the baby knew all about smiling and winning hearts. Surely she was God's gift to a family sorely in need of a renewal of hope. Daniel loved to just sit holding the baby, smiling into the cherubic little face and crooning, "Oh, Mary, how like your mother you are," and he would say to the infant, "Can you believe I held your mama in my arms when she was just your size?" Hephzibah would listen to him dote on this adorable child and smile to herself at this tangible evidence of God's goodness. For her part, Hephzibah began weaving daydreams of finding cunning tiny tea sets for her little girl and joining her for tea parties with her stuffed dolls. She was likely to have a nursery full of them, for Daniel had already purchased several.

But never a day passed, scarcely even an hour, when the agony of loss did not impinge upon Hephzibah's mind, and she felt crushed under a backlog of sorrow. Often far into the night the grief would hit her afresh, and always upon waking — but a merciful God did allow time to soften the edges of her heartache, and she would mentally shake off the anguish and perform whatever task was demanding her attention. Sometimes she simply tried to ignore the pain that washed over her because she was used to it now.

Having a small baby did not deter her from trips to Charleston as frequently as she could manage them, for Hephzibah was becoming increasingly conscious of a persistent spiritual longing. The Sunday service messages at First Baptist seemed to consistently address the unspoken needs of her aching heart. Her need was difficult to articulate, for sometimes the soul knows for certain only that it is hungry. 'Rinthia as well came to count on these trips and began speaking of Charleston First Baptist as "our church."

Late in the year Hephzibah began making the trip back and forth on most Sundays. Some weeks there was no way to fit the trip in, and certainly it took the whole Sunday. If the weather was bad, Hephzibah chafed until the following week when she might be able to go again to Charleston.

Quite frequently in his messages, Richard Furman would make reference to the spirit of revival that had swept over much of the South, first in Kentucky and Tennessee and then on to the Carolinas. Furman often alluded to the period in the previous century that had come to be known as the Great Awakening, and he likened the current sense of renewal to a Second Great Awakening. Especially among Baptists, large numbers of slaves had come to saving faith, and Dr. Furman was particularly concerned about the spiritual welfare of the many enslaved men and women in their state.

Hephzibah noted that Furman was disturbed by those who spoke of slaves as merely property and overlooked the importance of their souls. He began actively evangelizing the slave population, and scores of enslaved men and women had professed their faith and been baptized into the membership of First Baptist

Charleston. For Hephzibah, it went without saying that the servants who rowed her to and from church on Sundays would also attend the services. Will and Jeffrey made the trip regularly and were leaders among the boatmen. Isaac and Joseph also made the trip most weeks, and John and his brother Hercules did as well. Hercules was well-named, for his strong arms helped speed the small boat through the waters along the coastline. Hephzibah looked forward to hearing the Gullah chants they would sing in the form of rounds, the liquid words and rhythms like a soothing lullaby. She whiled away the long hours on the little boat by praying and meditating, finding solace in the rhythmic sound of the waves hitting the boat as it sliced through the water and in the voices of the men singing in harmony.

It was not just among men and women who were slaves, but for many of the inhabitants of the low country a sense of revival was spreading. Hephzibah personally sought to understand more of how to serve God and how to grow in grace. The more she studied and learned, the more her yearnings grew. She felt that old irrepressible ache to know what her point in the world might be. The seeking young mother could not articulate, even in her inner thoughts, just why she had found so much more food for her soul in the times of worship at the Baptist church. It was simply that way. This was also something of a sore spot for Daniel. Here he was, a leader at Edisto's Presbyterian church, yet his wife only attended with him sporadically and refused to become a member. It remained one of several points on which the couple could not see eye to eye.

Hephzibah's certainty that she was pregnant again arrived

about the time 1805 rolled around. Townsend was delighted, but Hephzibah's emotions were a tangle. She looked forward to this child, but so much had happened with so many of her babies that her joy was mixed with trepidation. Not caring this time whether the child would be a boy or a girl, she simply prayed for a healthy child and entreated God to spare the life of this new babe and let it grow to adulthood. Hephzibah Townsend was not yet twenty-five and had already given birth to seven babies; only two were still living.

Meanwhile, her sisters 'Rinthia and Martha were studying regularly with John Ferrars' tutor, and 'Rinthia was also spending a great deal of time assisting Hephzibah in duties around the house and plantation, rather like on-the-job training for the life she would likely lead when she herself married one day. As for her young servant Bella, she was assuming more and more of the duties in the kitchen, and Jane was glad to allow her added responsibilities, for rheumatism was causing grief to the old cook's joints. Bella reveled in her role as assistant cook and beamed with pride the night she cooked the entire meal and Jane was complimented on the excellent cooking. Jane gave one of her rare smiles and announced to the family that her assistant in the kitchen had prepared it all.

John was six and Mary Frampton a year-and-a-half-old toddler when Hephzibah went into labor on the morning of August 25, 1805. This would be her eighth baby, but each birth was like a renewed miracle. Late that sultry summer evening, Hephzibah gave birth to Susan Martha Townsend, who came with her mother's dark hair and her father's blue eyes. Mary Frampton was a bit too young to feel that her nose was out of joint and she quickly adjusted to having a tiny one in the nursery. Maum Nancy thrived on having another baby to care for, and Hephzibah often smiled to hear her crooning some of the same Gullah lullabies that she herself had learned from Maum Jean. In point of fact, Hephzibah always felt a sense of the presence of her beloved Maum Jean when she was in the nursery. An essential part of Hephzibah's character was bound up in the investments that slave woman had made in shaping her life.

By the time baby Susan was about six months old, Hephzibah had formed the habit of making the round trip to Charleston nearly every weekend. A disgruntled Townsend was not happy with Hephzibah's travels, but his wife was in no way deterred by this lack of approval. Those Sunday services had become something very important to her, and her resoluteness remained steadfast. For his part, Dr. Furman was impressed with her determination and with her consistent desire for him to come occasionally to Edisto to preach. Late that year, Furman began coming on an infrequent Saturday to the island. The local Episcopal congregation graciously allowed their sanctuary to be used for the islanders who gathered to hear the well-known Baptist minister. On those occasional weekends, Hephzibah considered that Saturday was her Sunday, and various friends and plantation owners attended those infrequent services along with her and many of the servants.

Throughout the coming year, a busy Hephzibah Townsend raised her little ones, ran the plantation with practiced ease and continued attending Sunday services in Charleston. A resigned Daniel Townsend shook his head and saved his breath to cool his porridge; Hephzibah would do what Hephzibah wanted to do. Had he not at least learned that in the past ten years? That indomitable force of character had simply grown stronger with the passing of the years. The trip by boat usually took six hours each way, depending on the weather, and that was a total of twelve hours that Hephzibah considered time well spent. The faithful servants who made this trip each week were benefiting along with their mistress, as they, too, received spiritual sustenance in those worship services. There was never a question of whether or not they would attend with Miz Hephzibah. That was understood.

The slaves sat in the gallery that ran along the sides and back of the sanctuary. In every church that Hephzibah had attended since the time she was born, there had been a slave gallery, but she never looked at a gallery without wondering why this was. Could not people worshipping God do so seated side by side, no matter what color their skin? She only asked these questions in her own mind now, for when she had voiced this query, all she ever got was a puzzled stare, as if such a thought was unheard of.

Since the time that Hephzibah had begun making those Sunday trips a regular practice, she had rented a pew at First Baptist. 'Rinthia sat with her and occasionally one of their Charleston relatives was in attendance and joined them in the pew. Hephzibah often smiled to herself as she thought how simple it was for Dr. Furman to see who of his congregation was in attendance on any given Sunday; all he had to do was glance at the family pews.

The membership of First Baptist was accustomed to the presence of Mrs. Townsend by this time, but a few who did not know the Edisto family sometimes wondered at the air of sadness she often wore like a cloak. Not only was 'Rinthia now a regular on Sundays but Martha as well. By the time 1807 arrived, Hephzibah had determined that it was time for her to be immersed and to become officially a part of the Charleston congregation. When she told Daniel of her decision, his face looked thunderous. "Is not our Edisto church good enough for you?" was his immediate response.

"Daniel, I must do what I feel God wants me to do," Hephzibah countered. "Can you not understand that? It isn't that the Presbyterian church isn't good enough," she continued. "It is just that my heart tells me I must follow God's guidance for me." Townsend shook his head with resignation, "Hephzibah, just do what you must do. You will anyway!" Hephzibah sensed that male pride might be at work here, and determined on her part to be as cooperative as she could in supporting Daniel in his efforts at the Presbyterian church. Hopefully that would make him more accepting of her decision.

On the following Sunday's trip to Charleston, Hephzibah met with Dr. Furman after the morning service and told him of her decision. Furman had known Hephzibah Townsend since she had been Hephzibah Jenkins and had seen her faith blossom and mature. It was one of the highlights of the year 1807 for Hephzibah Townsend when she was baptized into the fellowship of Charleston's First Baptist Church. At the same time she made her decision, several of the slaves who had made the trip those many Sundays had come to faith as well. Furman had the pleasure of baptizing several of them that same day. All the hours of the long trip back to Edisto, Hephzibah reflected on the deep soul satisfaction that had come with this signal event in her life. It felt like the beginning of a new chapter in her life, as indeed it turned out to be.

— *Sixteen* —

1809-1810
POLLY WEBB AND THE MITE SOCIETY

The sun peeped out suddenly from between the racing clouds and shone through the nursery window on a cozy scene of two little girls seated with their fond mother and friends who had come for their dolly tea party. Young Mary Frampton admonished four-year-old Susan Martha to "be very careful with your cup of tea!" Susan very slowly lifted the tiny porcelain cup with its dainty rosebuds to her lips and took a satisfying sip. The girls had carefully placed their stuffed dolls around the tiny table and were serving "tea and crumpets" to the dolls as well as their other guests. 'Rinthia and Martha entered into the spirit of the tea party, and Hephzibah reveled in such moments. These were treasures to capture in her memory and store away to be taken out and enjoyed for a long time to come.

Bella scratched at the door and stuck her head in to see if "the dish of crumpets needed refilling." She had baked the tiny treats for the little ones and could not imagine anything more satisfying than to watch the children playing grownups. Bella's skills were growing apace, and she was now a skilled cook at the ripe old age of eighteen. Hephzibah never looked at the young slave without thinking of how proud Maum Jean would be to see her great-niece thriving and learning.

Maum Nancy had faithfully followed in her Aunt Maum Jean's footsteps, and was right there in the nursery for the tea party. The little girls adored Maum Nancy and hung onto her wonderful stories that lulled them to sleep at night. Hephzibah smiled to recall the evening she had gone into the nursery to tuck the children in and heard Maum Nancy bowing to their entreaties to "tell us about the people who could fly" once more. It was their favorite folk tale, and they never seemed to tire of hearing it. Maum Jean had passed the tale on to Nancy, as all such Gullah bits of folklore were kept alive. Hearing the tale again brought back to Hephzibah memories of her own childhood and Maum Jean telling her the very same story.

Hephzibah could almost see Old Toby whispering to the young slave Sarah as she labored in the fields — Sarah, with her baby strapped to her back and trying so hard to do her hoeing, even as the wicked overseer yelled and cracked his whip, cutting into her legs. Old Toby was one of the "magic" ones who could fly. Although he had to leave his wings behind in West Africa, the magic came with him and he hurt to see Sarah's suffering. After the cruel overseer turned his back, Sarah whispered to old Toby, "Now, Father, help me now before it too late," and Toby said, "Yes, Daughter!" and he raised his arms and whispered, "Kum … yali, kum buba tambe," and up, up, up went Sarah, over the treetops, up to the clouds, and flew away to freedom. Back on the ground sat two little girls, large-eyed in wonder as they heard with a satisfaction that never grew old how Sarah and her baby were now safe and free and flying away.

'Rinthia and Martha as well particularly enjoyed being part

of the nursery ritual, for it reminded them of special times when they themselves had been little girls. It was hard to believe but 'Rinthia was already eighteen and showed no interest yet in any of the young men from nearby plantations, a number of whom were quite clearly interested in her. It was easy to see, even to a casual observer, that she and Hephzibah were sisters. 'Rinthia was a bit taller but their eyes were very similar and their smiles nearly identical. Looking at Hephzibah, with her complexion as fresh as this morning's biscuits, no one could imagine she was already a matronly twenty-nine years old. Their younger sister, Martha, was seventeen now and she, as well, promised to be another beauty. Her hair was lighter in shade, with golden glints, but she, too, had the "Jenkins" beautiful dark eyes.

John Ferrars disdained tea parties in the nursery. After all, he was ten years old now. After mornings with his tutor, he delighted in getting outdoors. Townsend expected him to spend some time each week learning about running a plantation, but John managed to find time most days to get with one of his pals from a neighboring plantation and fish or swim or do any of the things that occupy the mind of an inquisitive and growing boy. Daniel Townsend lost no occasion, however, in reminding his son that one day "all this will be yours" and that he had a big responsibility and much to learn. For her part, Hephzibah was concerned about some of the attitudes she noticed developing in her son, but she also noted that always he treated her with respect and devotion, and that encouraged her heart. At the same time, she feared she was having precious little influence on his way of thinking.

Life had been calmer in the past two years than at any time

since Hephzibah's marriage to Daniel some thirteen years earlier. From the time of her baptism in 1807, three years after the great drowning tragedy that had taken the lives of so many dear to her, she had managed to gain a calmer perspective on life. Calm did not mean complacent, however. Hephzibah constantly felt a gnawing sense of something left undone, an ever-present feeling of needing to know what she should do with her life that could make a difference. She so often felt crushed under a backlog of sorrow, having lost so many little ones, then her parents, and then on top of that, her beloved brother as well as dear Thomas and Richard. Many a night she agonized and cried out in her mind, *Oh God, how do I deal with sorrow this intense?*

Thank God for the healing power of time. Then, following her affiliation with the Charleston church, she experienced a new sense of belonging. *Strange,* she would often think, *it is as if my heart has found its resting spot.* Now she wanted to learn and grow and find that purpose in the world God had for her. Hephzibah Townsend could not know how God was going to use her life as a catalyst to involve future generations in ministry.

The busy mother began to make time each night before bed to have a quiet time with her Bible. Scripture took on an all-new meaning to her as she studied various passages and meditated on their deeper truths. She and Daniel had faithfully continued the habits of her childhood home and had family devotions each evening, but her personal time of study was becoming an enriching and encouraging oasis in a busy life for the mistress of Bleak Hall.

Hephzibah reread the account in the Gospel of John about the

Samaritan woman, and it seemed to take on a fresh new meaning for her. Here was the rabbi named Jesus who talked of theology with a mere woman, speaking with her as a person who had her own identity. Hephzibah had always heard about the Samaritan woman being "bad," with all those husbands, but it dawned on her that Jesus took seriously this woman's mind and opinions and questions. And then, the people in that community had believed because of *her* testimony. It was like a revelation to Hephzibah. Certainly women in Bible times had had no more status than those in nineteenth-century America, but look how the Lord used a nameless woman of Samaria. Consequently, Hephzibah began to consider with real seriousness what God might have in mind for her, personally, to do.

For several years now, Dr. Furman led Saturday "Baptist services" on Edisto every two or three months as his time permitted. It was a particular joy to Hephzibah when 'Rinthia came to make her public profession of faith and asked Dr. Furman for baptism. It was as if her own child had come to faith, and in a way that was true, for Hephzibah had been much the mother figure in 'Rinthia's life from the time of her birth.

The Edisto Episcopal congregation continued to prove helpful in allowing the meetings to be held in their building, and Hephzibah saw to it that the Townsend servants were able to attend. It was mostly the house servants who were regular in attendance, as Daniel had little patience with "free time" for the slaves. It was simply another sore spot for the couple, who sometimes managed to handle their differences of opinion with more grace than others. Hephzibah felt especially proprietary about those servants who had come from the Jenkins plantation with her, and such thinking found little favor with her husband. The Townsends mostly tried not to openly air their disagreements but did not always succeed.

Bella was faithful in attendance at those Saturday services and was growing deep in her faith. Hephzibah rejoiced when she, along with Maum Nancy and several others of the household staff, professed faith and were baptized by Pastor Furman. Hephzibah began to recognize that it was often around two particular issues that she and Daniel most frequently disagreed. One, of course, was money — always a sore spot, for Hephzibah viewed it as belonging to both of them. After all, she had brought much of it to the marriage. The other bone of contention was their slaves and how they should be regarded. The number of their slave population had increased quite dramatically because Sea Island Cotton was very labor-intensive. This was their major crop, and many hands were needed. Townsend handled everything about the process strictly like a business, with little time spent reflecting on the moral issues or the importance of considering a slave's feelings. On one point, however, Townsend did defer to Hephzibah's strongly held view that families must not be separated. On that she would not budge, never mind that it was often not economically expedient.

Hephzibah simply could not dismiss a living person as business. She observed and listened and read much on the subject and found it increasingly disturbing. And just as frequently, she felt alone on an island in her feelings about the justness of slavery. As a child, she frequently heard about the great Henry Laurens, that wealthy slave owner who had himself bought and sold many slaves but then had come to abhor the practice. She was stirred by the realization that upon his death, Laurens freed his slaves, as did his son John.

Sometimes Hephzibah deplored her own cowardice in not following the promptings of her heart. It did no good to tell herself that as a married woman in nineteenth-century America, she had precious few legal rights. This did little to calm her heart or soothe her conscience. Nonetheless, there continued to grow in her a determination to do something about justice and right in her own small way, and she actually prayed for the wisdom to know just what moves she might make. Always ringing in Hephzibah's heart were the words of her beloved nurse the night she died. It resounded like an echo. She kept hearing Maum Jean saying that her body might be a slave but her mind was free, and then whispering that, for Miz Hephzibah, it was the opposite. Those words forever served as a goad to prick at her heart.

Then a new interest fired Hephzibah's imagination, when, in his sermon one Sunday in Charleston, Dr. Furman told of the need to spread the gospel around the world. Somehow she had never thought much about the world beyond their own horizons, but as Furman explained the challenge of Christ's command to His disciples to "go into all the world," it dawned on her for the first time that this command did not have a time limit. Surely it must be a command to her personally just as much as it was for the disciples those thousands of years earlier.

Dr. Furman seemed to have missions on his mind, for on several successive Sundays he told of needs in faraway lands. Hephzibah thrilled to hear about the pioneer missionary from

India who had braved the oceans to go to India, where millions of souls had never heard of God and His love. William Carey had been just a humble shoe cobbler, and yet God had led him to share the good news with people of another race, people who had no idea of a sovereign God. Dr. Carey was even now translating Scripture into an incredibly complex language, and Hephzibah grew excited just hearing reports from India. She was becoming increasingly aware that Furman was a pioneer among Baptists, one who was leading out in urging a missions consciousness among fellow believers. Hephzibah always had those long Sunday evening hours in the boat returning to Edisto to meditate on Furman's message and its meaning for her life.

Mrs. Townsend was particularly excited the morning she heard Dr. Furman tell of a little paraplegic woman in Boston who had organized a mite society to pray for missionaries and to raise money to support their work. She was struck with the realization that if Polly Webb — a woman who could not even walk but had to get around in a wheelchair — could organize and lead a group of women to give and to pray and to help around the world, couldn't an able-bodied woman on a little island in South Carolina do much the same thing? Maybe this was part of the answer to that nagging yearning in her to find out how God could use her to make a difference.

As the new year arrived, Hephzibah was mulling over in her mind just how she might be able to make some sort of impact in a world that seemed far beyond her reach. She began talking with 'Rinthia about her impressions. Her sister had heard those same messages at First Baptist and found Hephzibah's idea intriguing.

By tacit consent, they discussed their views and ideas in those moments when just the two of them had some time together. Both young women realized that this concept of the Great Commission might appear far-fetched to folk who had never even considered such far-reaching challenges for people in America — say nothing of women.

By the time February 1810 arrived, Hephzibah knew with certainty that she was going to have another child. Daniel actually seemed a bit surprised when she told him the news. It was the first time in five years she had greeted him with such tidings. This had been the longest span in their married life in which Hephzibah had not given birth, and both were quite excited about a new baby. This time around, young John Ferrars was determined that this baby would be a brother, whereas Mary Frampton and Susan Martha asked Mommy for a sister. Hephzibah was happy to tell her children that she would show no partiality whatsoever, but instead leave the choice up to the good Lord.

~ *Seventeen* ~

1810

BELLA

Even as Hephzibah grew increasingly delighted with the prospect of another baby, so grew her excitement over the possibilities that might be available to begin something wholly new. Why not form a group of women in the low country who could make an impact in many other countries? Surely if a handicapped woman with few resources could organize and guide a group of committed ladies to effect change on distant shores, then a woman with more resources plus a hefty helping of intestinal fortitude should also be able to make a meaningful contribution. Young Mrs. Townsend did not delude herself that her own resources were going to be readily available, however. They had certainly not been, all these some fourteen years of married life. And yet, she was never one to despair and give up without a try. Force of character would surely come to the fore yet again. With the passing of the years, so grew that strength of character both in intensity and depth.

Hephzibah noted how easily she tired these days, but reminded herself that no longer was she a teenage mother-to-be, but a thirty-year-old woman whose body had already been through eight pregnancies. Furthermore, the plethora of tasks that fell her way on a daily basis did not lessen just because her body was becoming increasingly unwieldy. Yet over everything grew the sense of anticipation she felt about the new project evolving in her mind and heart. 'Rinthia was a terrific sounding board, less creative than her older sister, yet very level-headed and practical, a young woman who faced life with common sense and a healthy dose of realism. The sisters discussed other women of their acquaintance, many of whom were cousins in one way or another, who might respond to just such a challenge. Some were Baptist and many were Presbyterian and Episcopalian, but each had a caring heart and would likely be interested in something so new and unusual.

By mutual agreement, Hephzibah and 'Rinthia decided to discuss their ideas first with Aunt Abby. With her advancing years, their aunt had slowed down considerably, but nothing slowed down her mental acuity. Loyal Presbyterian that she was, Abby had a heart that encompassed just about everyone, and she was intrigued with what these two young women were considering. As always, she added a dash of practicality to the recipe and made some pragmatic suggestions. Among her queries was the question to Hephzibah about how to put her hands on the money necessary for such an endeavor. Abby gave a wry smile as she also suggested to Hephzibah that she might try a bit of patience in dealing with her husband regarding money for missions. For her part, however, Hephzibah never was one to regard patience as much of a virtue.

Ever hopeful, young Mrs. Townsend determined yet again to approach Daniel and see what could be done about loosening the purse strings. They were usually quite tightly drawn, but no one could ever honestly accuse Hephzibah Townsend of timidity or cowardice. Daniel would clearly be her first avenue of approach toward needed funds.

Hephzibah tried to look for a quiet moment after supper when no one else was around to approach Daniel on the subject that had taken hold of her mind. Such moments were not easy to come by on a large and bustling plantation. That April evening, Hephzibah found her moment and began waxing eloquent about what she had learned from Dr. Furman concerning the mite society in Boston, and even more so about William Carey and what was happening among the heathen in India. Townsend listened with a marked lack of interest, although he was courteous enough to hear her out. "Daniel," she finally came to a pause and declared, "I need some funds to begin this endeavor; it is simply vital that Dr. Carey have resources for this translation work, which is proving so successful." She plunged ahead, not giving serious consideration to the fact that few wives would dare mention such a delicate subject to the head of the household. Hephzibah did not conform to the typical and proper image of a meek and submissive low country wife. "I feel," she stated, "like this would surely be a worthy use of some of the money that I brought to our marriage."

Daniel, however, was very much the typical plantation head of the household. "Hephzibah," he responded categorically, "it may well be that Dr. Carey is a great man and doing a great work. And Dr. Carey, my dear," he continued in a tone taken by his very determined wife to be nothing if not patronizing, "would no doubt applaud your good heart, but we have all sorts of people with all sorts of needs right here close to home. You just do good here," he admonished, as if concluding a lecture, "and I'm sure

God will be pleased."

"And, Husband," retorted his wife, whose always small store of patience was by now too sorely tried, "I am sure God will be pleased with my doing what He tells me in the Scripture I should do!" And assuming what dignity she could muster, Mrs. Townsend, with exaggerated politeness, concluded, "I bid you goodnight, Mr. Townsend, and I will find a way to do what I need to do," upon which she exited the room with a decided swish of her long skirts.

Seething over Daniel's enormities, but never one to quickly despair, Hephzibah immediately began focusing on ways to produce some discretionary income. Options on Edisto Island were extremely limited for plantation mistresses wanting to raise some funds on their own. Heaven forbid that a lady would work. Limited options, however, did not imply impossible options — not to Hephzibah Jenkins Townsend. She smiled to herself, recalling how Papa had told his little daughter long ago that she should always "put on her thinking cap" if she had a serious matter to contemplate. Papa's daughter decided this certainly qualified in the category of serious. And the first order of business was to consider her available resources. Immediately, her mind jumped to thoughts of Shargould, doubly precious to her because Brother had willed that property to her. There it sat, right next to Bleak Hall. On the heels of this thought came the idea of utilizing the talents of her own dear Bella. That young servant was a genius at cooking, especially producing pastries, and specialty baking was always in demand.

Consequently, Hephzibah managed to find a quiet moment

the next afternoon to pull Bella aside and propose a grand new idea to the quick-witted young woman. Would she be interested in learning some special baking skills, even beyond her usual excellent cakes, pies and puddings? Would she be interested in helping many people? Indeed Bella would, but it startled her to learn that Miz Hephzibah wanted to send her to Charleston to learn new ways of baking from Henri, the leading pastry chef at an exclusive restaurant located quite near the Townsends' house. Only about two times in all her eighteen years had Bella been to the big city, and it sounded scarily exciting to the young slave woman. Bella assured Miz Hephzibah she could have the kitchen duties here at Bleak Hall well covered while she was away and her own mama, Maum Grace, would see to its running smoothly. It was tacitly understood between the two of them, mistress and servant, that a smoothly run kitchen would keep the master of the home happy, and that was important.

The Charleston house remained staffed with help year-round, so Bella would have a safe place to stay while in the big city. Hephzibah realized that her lifelong relationship with this young servant was not a usual one, but then Hephzibah's birth had not been a usual one, and Bella was part of her own heart's attachment to her beloved Maum Jean. Hephzibah had been conscious of this special bond ever since Bella's birth. There wasn't a moment's doubt as to Bella's ability to speedily learn new skills. Accordingly, Hephzibah sent word to Chef Henri, along with a generous donation, and plans were underway within the month. An eager Bella left for Charleston early one Sunday morning, accompanying Miz Hephzibah as she made her weekly boat trip to church services. This meant an excited young Bella also attended the worship at First Baptist and heard Dr. Furman, a rare treat indeed.

Having explained her new scheme to 'Rinthia, the two of them the week before went early one morning to Shargould, taking along about four of the trusted young servants that Hephzibah knew she could count on. The plan was soon underway; right here at Shargould, the servants began using tabby to construct two large outdoor ovens very close to the shore on Frampton's Inlet. The cool breezes off the water would help make the heat coming from the ovens bearable, and within a month, the young men constructed two sturdy ovens from the local materials that made up tabby — a fine mixture of crushed oyster shells, sand, lime and water. The Townsend servants were justly proud of their new construction, and when Bella returned from Charleston, Hephzibah's "mission business" could begin.

Thankfully, Daniel was too busy with crops and business deals to pay much attention to Hephzibah's activities during the day. In addition to supervising work at Bleak Hall Plantation, Townsend also spent a great deal of time supervising his Wadmalaw plantations and handling business interests in Charleston. As long as their household was running smoothly, he assumed that all was well. The Townsends were maintaining something of a polite truce those days, neither alluding to the domestic fracas that sent Hephzibah off in such a huff a couple of months ago. Daniel decided that his wife had come to her senses and forgotten her grandiose ideas about involving herself with people half a world away. For his part, he determined not to bring the subject up, but rather to let it wither away.

Expecting a baby within months, running a large and complex plantation home, raising three active children, and bearing responsibility for several hundred lives did not daunt the intrepid young mistress of Bleak Hall who was now thirty. Several Sundays she was not able to make the trip to Charleston, but thankfully Dr. Furman was able to come to Edisto about one Saturday a month and that served to encourage her heart. She was yet to broach this mite society idea to her pastor, but she and 'Rinthia now made some initial visits to cousins and friends on neighboring plantations. The sisters let the ladies know something new was in the offing, something they, too, might be able to be part of. Hephzibah was only hinting and giving no details.

There was Eliza Adams, one of Hephzibah's Wadmalaw friends and a distant relative. As well, there was Aunt Abby's daughter-in-law, Martha Mary, who had been a Meggett until she married Abby's son Joseph. Then there was Phoebe Edings, along with Martha Seabrook and two or three more friends. Hephzibah promised her cousins and friends that, very soon now, she wanted to introduce them to some new ideas and explain how they were going to be able to be pathfinders. For young women and older ones as well whose lives had been almost totally circumscribed and governed by tradition, the idea of doing something unusual and meaningful quite captured their imaginations. Furthermore, Hephzibah had them very curious by this time.

Bella returned from Charleston full of enthusiasm and justly proud of her new expertise with specialty cakes. Her pride and joy was the creative gingerbread recipe taught her by Chef Henri, surely the most moist and tender gingerbread ever whipped up.

Bella's excitement knew no bounds when she saw the bright, new, white tabby ovens right there on the inlet. She had never seen the like. And Hephzibah herself never went to Shargould without feeling a special sense of the presence of Brother, knowing without doubt that he would applaud such unique use of the property he had passed on to Sister.

Now was the time to begin; Hephzibah was anxious to get started, for her baby was due in a couple of months. Bella made sure all was going smoothly in the kitchen of Bleak Hall that first morning, and then supervised the loading of cooking supplies and ingredients in one of the plantation carts. Hephzibah was on hand to watch the process begin, her sense of excitement on tiptoe. The dream was actually beginning. By afternoon, the heady fragrance of spices was emanating from the large ovens and making everyone nearby hungry for a taste. The first cake out of the large ovens was ceremoniously cut and shared by mistress and servants alike, and applauded as perfectly delicious.

Hephzibah had been thinking for months about just how to conduct the sales. Charleston was the likely market, with plenty of customers for specialty baked goods offered fresh from the oven and at reasonable prices. Consequently, after several days of baking, she once again planned a quiet evening chat with Daniel. Shortly after a satisfying dinner, and with the children off to bed after family devotions, she broached the subject.

"Daniel," she began, "I've been doing some baking over at Shargould."

"Baking? Baking at Shargould? What put this particular bee in your bonnet?" Daniel was startled.

"I recall," Hephzibah proceeded, "that you did not wish to release funds for missions endeavors, so I decided not to trouble you further. However, I've been able to have some baking done," and then she paused to take a breath. "And I am planning to have several of the servants take the goods to Charleston on Saturday and sell them at the market." Townsend looked thunderstruck and retorted, "You have done what?" Patiently, Hephzibah repeated her plans, and this time Daniel responded almost before the words were out of her mouth, "Well, I'm not going to allow my servants to go to the market and sell!"

Those words seemed to somehow hang in the air and settle on her shoulders. Hephzibah had attempted to mentally prepare herself for just such a rejoinder, and had her response thought out. "That is all right, sir," she spoke as calmly as she could, "then I will plan to take them to market myself."

There flew to Daniel's mind a sudden picture of his lovely, young and very pregnant wife selling baked goods at the market in Charleston, the market frequented by many of their family and friends. He found the image a shocking one. The ensuing time of somewhat heated conversation was exhausting to both. Nevertheless, before they departed for bed that night, the Townsends' domestic difficulties had at least worked out to the point that Daniel was going to allow the servants to go and do the selling. Hephzibah went to sleep hugging a happy grin to her heart. Brother would have been so happy to see what a blessing Shargould was being, and she drifted off to sleep on the thought: *The Edisto missions endeavor is just about to be born.*

Original tabby ovens on Edisto Island in which Hephzibah baked her ginger-bread. (Tabby is a mixture of oyster shells, lime and water.) On the National Register of Historic Places.

~ *Eighteen* ~

1810
THE TALE OF THE TABBY OVENS

The occasional clink of a delicate porcelain tea cup being placed in its saucer mingled with the gentle murmur of some dozen voices, as ladies both young and not so young sat in the parlor of Bleak Hall catching up on the latest happenings on Edisto and Wadmalaw and the most current news from Charleston. The spacious parlor was bright with color from the long, flowing skirts of low country plantation mistresses out for a morning visit. With many of the plantations on Edisto and Wadmalaw widely scattered, it was a rare treat for this many women to be able to get together for the purpose of enjoying one another in the midst of busy summer days. Eliza Adams from Wadmalaw took special pleasure in chatting with her longtime friend Abby Mikell; the two had not been able to visit for several months, and the atmosphere of goodwill, a cool breeze from the open windows of the parlor and the delicious gingerbread and fancy cakes being served all added special touches to the gathering.

On the minds of most was the intriguing question of why Hephzibah Townsend had assembled such a group. All the tantalizing hints of something new in the air had everyone curious. 'Rinthia, of course, was well aware of the reason for the occasion, as was Martha; the two young Jenkins sisters were assisting

Hephzibah in making friends and relatives feel welcomed and comfortable. After the general excitement of seeing old friends again and learning the latest news, Hephzibah gracefully rose, as gracefully as a woman seven months expectant could rise, and stood near the mantel under the beautiful gleaming mirror that hung on the wall behind.

Welcoming them as a group, Hephzibah launched into her account of what she had learned in the past few months, telling of the remarkable news she had gleaned from the eminent Dr. Furman about William Carey in India and how he was translating the Scripture for the heathen. Her eyes sparkled as she related the account of what God was doing so far away. Then she recounted the story of Polly Webb and her mite society in Boston. Hephzibah described the young paraplegic and her group of friends who were influencing lives around the world through praying and giving. Occasionally, one of the women would pose a question as to how on earth Miss Webb did this or that, or how Dr. Carey could do his work in such a difficult place.

Hephzibah responded to questions from all around, enjoying seeing a gleam of interest on one face after another, as they heard their friend intimate that they, too, might be able to make a difference. "But, Hephzibah," spoke up Martha Murray, "you know how little ready money we ladies have." She looked puzzled, "I don't see how we can do something like that here in the low country." Several women murmured agreement, and Hephzibah grinned and raised her brows. "Ladies," she responded, "let's take a brief tour." And one woman after another looked around in bewilderment. A tour? Today?

Hephzibah had planned well, for standing in front of Bleak Hall were the two finest carriages on the plantation, ready to take the ladies on their brief mystery journey. A dozen chattering women were handed into the carriages and were off down the avenue of oaks headed in the direction of Shargould Plantation, situated nearby on Frampton's Inlet. And even as the carriages turned left down the driveway leading to nearby Shargould, the most delicious fragrance came wafting through the air — gingerbread! Fresh gingerbread. Everyone was all-attention as Hephzibah and 'Rinthia led the way to a pair of gleaming, new, white outdoor tabby ovens, where servants were busy putting in and taking out pans of gingerbread. Aunt Abby exclaimed in amazement, "Hephzibah Jenkins Townsend, what in the world is going on here!"

Hephzibah was smiling broadly by this time, and she called out to the young woman directing the work. "Bella," she requested, "come meet these ladies who are visiting Bleak Hall today."

"And, ladies," she addressed the group, "I want you to meet the baking wizard. This is Bella," Hephzibah introduced the young servant, "Bella is the one who has produced these wonderful cakes and breads." Bella was beaming as she thanked the women who were commenting on the remarkably tender gingerbread they were now sampling, unlike any they had ever tasted. Trying to answer a dozen questions fired one after another, Hephzibah finally protested, "All right, all right, I'd love to tell you the story. Let's go back to Bleak Hall and continue our meeting," she suggested.

Settled back in the parlor of Bleak Hall, Hephzibah was

peppered with a score of questions, and, asking the women to be seated, began to tell the tale of the ovens and the idea that had been brewing in her mind for months now. 'Rinthia chimed in with explanations, as well, as the two of them expounded on the possibilities of what a small group of women might do to really make a difference. Hephzibah was glowing as she told how, at market last Saturday, there had been a profit at the end of the day of a dollar and seventy-five cents. To women with precious little discretionary money, it sounded munificent. The imaginations of a dozen minds went to work as each began to envision how she, a busy woman with much to do and limited personal funds, might also be able to contribute. Listening to Hephzibah was like a revelation. *Maybe I could do something similar* was the thought entering many minds. "But, Hephzibah," Phoebe Edings spoke up, "what would *I* do? You know how difficult it is for us as wives to get our hands on funds of our own. And we don't have a Shargould property willed to us by a brother as a resource, either," she added with a grimace.

"Nor do we have a Bella who is a baking genius," added Martha Seabrook, ever practical.

"Ah yes," Hephzibah agreed. "But, Martha, I know you are an expert in producing those wonderful English lavender soaps that you made and gave as Christmas gifts last year."

Martha looked pleased, "Why, so I did," she considered. "Now that might be something I could do to help missions causes."

Hephzibah clapped her hands in delight, "Wonderful idea, Martha. And let me tell you ladies how the breads and cakes are producing funds, and it might give all of us some ideas."

Proceeding to explain how the gingerbread and cakes were made during the weekdays and then taken early Saturday morning to market in Charleston, she could see the women looking at one another and nodding as if to say, *maybe there's an idea here for me as well.*

"Ladies," Martha Murray chimed in, "I have a feeling that each of us can come up with a plan on which we can hang our bonnets as well." All smiled as they pictured their proverbial bonnets hanging on some innovative new source of income, at which point Hephzibah suggested they take time to pray and ask God's blessings on the new mission endeavors of Dr. Carey and on their planning as well. As a group, they earnestly sought God's guidance to show them how to proceed in this new venture that was fast taking hold of their hearts and imaginations.

Aunt Abby's prayer for God's strength and wisdom nearly brought several in the group to tears, as they realized their utter dependence on Providence to guide even their thinking. And then the ideas began to flow. Martha Mary thought of the oils she had developed for seasonings and even some for medicinal purposes. Phoebe remembered the beautiful crocheted buttons that were her pride and joy. She loved giving them for gifts to friends at Christmas, and it was easy to make them quickly in the evenings while sitting in the parlor with the family gathered round. Eliza Adams recalled the wonderful fragrant talcum power and skin products an elderly servant woman had taught her to make years earlier there on her Wadmalaw plantation. These might find a great market in Charleston as well. The more the ladies talked, the more ideas that tumbled out and the more excited they grew.

Hephzibah Townsend was nothing if not persuasive, and her force of character was revealing itself afresh in her ability to relate to her friends and fire their creativity. The group decided to start off by meeting once every two months, since travel was quite difficult for a group who lived so far apart. Each lady left that afternoon with a specially wrapped package of Bella's ginger-bread to share with her family and a mind teeming with ideas and enthusiasm. Little did they realize that they were actually the beginning of a massive movement among women of the South, one that would endure.

Just weeks away from delivering her ninth baby, Hephzibah was completely exhausted by bedtime, but her excitement could scarcely contain itself over the evident blessings God had showered on the day. Pray God it would catch hold and she could help make some sort of eternal difference. It could be that this was part of her point in the world. As she parted from 'Rinthia and Martha that night, the two of them were already hard at work figuring out just how they could be part of the mission giving. Martha had a wonderful way with herbs, and 'Rinthia had learned how to make a fragrant soothing lip balm. It should go well in Charleston's open market.

Within two weeks of the first meeting of the women, Hephzibah went into labor and the family waited anxiously for its newest member. Maum Grace had developed into a competent midwife, and Hephzibah was grateful for her support and encouragement. 'Rinthia didn't leave her sister's side, bathing her forehead in soothing lavender water and letting her squeeze her hands tightly as the pains increased. Practice didn't make perfect in having babies, a groaning Hephzibah concluded. After what seemed like an endless night, in the early hours before dawn on August 19, a beautiful baby girl vociferously announced her arrival. Daniel beamed in relief at his first sight of their newest child, and Hephzibah tiredly noted that their last three babies had all been girls.

Daniel, holding his precious newborn, observed that Baby needed a name. A weary but exhilarated Hephzibah responded, "Let's name her Amarinthia, after her aunt. That would mean much to me." Upon which Daniel tenderly handed the tiny infant into 'Rinthia's waiting arms, and the young aunt's eyes welled with tears as she held her namesake for the first time.

'Rinthia was also a topic of discussion and teasing at the dinner table a few weeks later, when Hephzibah commented on the special attention she had noticed young Mr. William Wilkerson of Charleston paying to her sister. 'Rinthia blushed but didn't protest. Hephzibah was actually quite pleased about Wilkerson, because her sister had evinced little interest in any of the young beaus who had attempted to woo her. Hephzibah hoped young William would bide his time and not rush her sister. She liked what she had learned of this young man. 'Rinthia was like a daughter to her, and Hephzibah had her interests very much at heart. Martha was younger, and had not seemed interested in any beau, so Hephzibah was hoping she would wait a bit. One at a time was enough.

The second ladies' meeting at Bleak Hall occurred in October, two months after the arrival of Amarinthia and young and old alike oohed and aahed over the tiny little black-haired girl who looked uncannily like her fond mama. The women were not disappointed to be served Bella's gingerbread once more, and there was much chatter about what ideas each had come up with for raising funds for missions endeavors. Phoebe Edings reported that her husband had lost the young man who had been doing the accounts for the plantation and she had hit on the clever idea of offering to do a "bit of accounting" for the plantation, and her husband picked up on it immediately. Phoebe was a deft hand with numbers, and she could be relied on to produce accurate and timely records. She, in turn, was delighted with her creative way to raise funds. One after another chimed in with reports and ideas, and after the group prayed for Dr. Carey and the missionaries in India, Hephzibah suggested they decide on a name for their society.

All agreed that they wished to be known as a "mite" society, but deciding on an actual name was not as simple. After all, most of the women were from Edisto Island, but then, a few were from Wadmalaw Island, which certainly should be recognized as well. Hephzibah diplomatically suggested that they become the "Wadmalaw-Edisto Female Mite Society," and a chorus of agreement met her idea. Hephzibah reported that she was planning to return to Sunday services in Charleston in the next week or so and was eager to inform Dr. Furman of what had occurred on the island. She also wanted to learn fresh news of Dr. Carey's work and also efforts among the Catawba Indians here in South Carolina. The ladies were already laying aside their money and were anxious to begin sending it to meet needs. In fact, each was feeling a bit like a pioneer, and it was a good feeling.

Tiny Amarinthia thrived from the start, and three months

following her birth, Hephzibah was able to make the arduous Sunday trip back to church in Charleston. She had sorely missed the fellowship and inspiration she always found there. She was also longing for the opportunity to tell Dr. Furman about the mite society. Following the morning service on a bright November day, Hephzibah was able to spend some time with her pastor, who in turn was eager to hear news from his faithful parishioner from Edisto. Furman's eyes widened in surprise to learn that Mrs. Townsend had not only given birth to a healthy young daughter, but that at about the same time, a ladies' group had been organized for the support of missions. It appeared his missions enthusiasm had caught fire on Edisto Island. Furman could not have been more delighted, and Hephzibah was eager to learn any fresh missions news that she could pass on to the ladies. For his part, Furman felt a deep sense of satisfaction that some of his own missions zeal had actually borne fruit right here close to home.

Shortly before leaving for the long boat trip home, Hephzibah turned to another subject very dear to her heart. "Dr. Furman," and she looked straight into his eyes, "I am very serious about our need of a church on Edisto. You coming occasionally on a Saturday is wonderful," she hastened to explain, "but we need so much more."

Furman looked thoughtful, "I can understand your eagerness, Sister Townsend, but you understand," he hesitated, wanting to be practical but not to sound discouraging, "the undertaking of establishing a church is a huge endeavor. You will recall there used to be a Baptist congregation on the island. There was land and a building that Baptists shared with other denominations. But," he continued, "the Episcopalians are renting out that land now and there is not a place to meet."

"Absolutely true," Hephzibah agreed, "but a church would not be impossible. There are so many needs, and I am concerned that our servants need steady spiritual guidance. There are a few other Baptists around the island," she noted, "but most don't have the time or will to make a boat trip each Sunday, for it takes the whole day. Pastor," Hephzibah concluded, "will you pray about this matter with me? I feel very strongly about this."

Furman agreed to pray over the idea in the days ahead, and Hephzibah spent the long trip home gazing out over the tranquil water and thinking about the possibilities of what God might do on her beloved Edisto. There had to be a way to make a church happen.

~ *Nineteen* ~

1811

A GROWING DREAM

Such dreams Hephzibah had, dreams for a Baptist church right here near home. Surely it wasn't impossible. Their fledgling new mite society had not waited on that vision of a church coming to fruition but had already taken on a life of its own. The Wadmalaw-Edisto Female Mite Society was plowing new soil for women in the South. Such an undertaking had never been attempted by anyone in this entire region, certainly not by a group made up solely of women. No doubt there would be plenty of naysayers when word about the society got out. After all, these were solely women who had organized; they were autonomous. No men were involved, and that alone was enough to garner criticism. Hephzibah spent little time in useless worries. However, it would not be the first time she had encountered criticism or censure, and no doubt, not the last.

It occurred to Hephzibah that she needed to learn a bit about the early Baptist church that had thrived on the island. She wanted to find out the current status of the land on which that church had been built. Dr. Furman had alluded to problems that might be involved with that property. Hephzibah discovered that Aunt Abby, of all people, had some information. Abby was a faithful Presbyterian, but her second husband, who had died just two years before, was both a direct descendant and a namesake of Ephraim Mikell, a strong Baptist pioneer who had willed that land plus an annual gift to a Baptist ministry on Edisto.

As Abby told the story, one time there had been a building on the land used jointly by Baptists and Presbyterians. Then, in about 1722, the Presbyterians, Abby grinned, managed through a strong pastor to take over the building. But right after that, Pastor William Tilly became the leader of the Baptist congregation and he himself lived on Edisto. The group flourished. They built a meeting place of their own and used it until the great majority of the members moved away from Edisto and became part of Euhaw Baptist Church. According to Aunt Abby's memory, the meeting house was still standing in about 1772, but somewhere between then and now it had disappeared.

The two women speculated on how heated the discussions must have been during those contentious times. Now, however, it appeared that the Episcopalians were receiving income from renting out that same property, so the land's history was a bit muddled, involving all three denominations. Before Ephraim died, he told Abby about the Episcopal church appealing to the state legislature for the right to use the land. However, there was a contingency put in the deed by his great-grandfather that kept them from getting title to it.

All this information gave Hephzibah a lot to contemplate. So there was land already, given in perpetuity to the Baptists of Edisto, but then those Baptists had largely moved away and the land was no longer considered theirs. A problem. But then, problems looked like challenges to Hephzibah Townsend, and this was simply a fresh challenge. She was determined that the dream could begin to move forward. Ever the realist, however, Hephzibah knew from the outset that Daniel would not be at all happy with the idea.

She was not wrong. When his wife first brought up the subject of an Edisto Baptist church, Townsend scoffed at the idea. "Hephzibah," he shook his head, "why on earth get into another project? You have already started a women's group that has no firm guidance from any male leader, making it shaky to begin with." A quick glance at his wife's face assured him that his comment was not well-received.

"Husband," she responded, "has our mite society suffered for lack of the guiding hand you are suggesting? We seem to be off to a firm start, in spite of thinking for ourselves," she concluded with a flourish.

"Possibly," Daniel retorted, "but there is no way a woman can begin a church on Edisto. Whoever heard of such a thing?"

So much for throwing down the gauntlet, which his wife immediately picked up. "And does that mean it cannot now be heard of?" she stated through pretty white teeth that were tightly clenched. "There are some other Baptists around Edisto. They would like to have a church nearer home, I have no doubt. And furthermore," Hephzibah was on a roll now, "I have been concerned for some time for so many of our servants. They are very seldom involved in worship services and they suffer from want of it. Their souls are equally important."

And here was another sore subject between the Townsends. Daniel was convinced that Hephzibah was far too indulgent with the slaves and spent too much time and effort on them, whereas Hephzibah looked upon this as her responsibility. Maum Jean's eyes were ever in the back of her mind, looking into her own eyes with loving concern. She was not going to abuse that trust. How many times had she pled with Daniel to understand, "These are my people"? And Daniel's response was usually a curt, "Nonsense!"

By this point Daniel was wound up. "Hephzibah, I am not happy about this, either your indulgence of our servants or your insistence on starting a Baptist church here on Edisto. And Wife, you are stretching the limits of what is proper," he concluded.

To which his maligned wife at once retorted, "And just who says it is not proper? I think it is proper — and I think I must do as I feel God wants me to do. And furthermore," she paused for breath, "I have a question to ask in return. Do you find that we have trouble with our servants because we provide some learning for them and treat them kindly?"

Daniel hesitated a moment before blustering in his reply, "Well, I realize that many of the servants came to you in your papa's will, but I still think you are too easy on them."

"Have you ever seen insubordination and surliness on our plantations, Daniel?" Hephzibah came back. As Daniel seemed to think over her question and slowly began shaking his head, she added, "Mr. Townsend, respect gains respect; everyone needs some dignity."

The subject was allowed to drop, but Hephzibah had no intention of dropping her dream. She could hear the echo of Papa's voice telling her so many times when she was small and struggling with something, "Sister, to him that will — ways are not wanting." His daughter seemed to have adopted that maxim as a way of life. Busy days revolved around the myriad tasks of a chatelaine supervising a large plantation household, mothering four active children, leading a growing group of women beginning a new ministry, and now planning how to start a church from the ground up. John Ferrars was twelve now, and busy with preparation for college in just a few short years. Mary and Susan were busy little girls, learning their letters and at the same time learning how to sew, embroider, knit and crochet, but always finding time to play and run around the yard and gardens just being children. Baby Amarinthia was doted on by young and old and thrived on the attention.

Bella, the baker, was now busier than ever. In addition to supervising the cooking at Bleak Hall, no small task, she oversaw the baking industry that was thriving over at Shargould. As if that were not enough, Bella now had a new shine in her eyes and another interest as well. One evening after a particularly excellent dinner topped off with a delicate new pastry recipe she had tried, Bella and her mistress found a few minutes for a quiet chat. Bella was a bit shy in revealing her secret, but wanted her beloved Miz Hephzibah to know and approve.

"Miz Hephzibah," Bella began, "you know Joseph, don't you, Joseph who builds furniture in the carpenter shop?"

"Of course, I do, Bella," Hephzibah responded, "Joseph came from the Jenkins plantation just as your family did. He was always one of the brightest in the schoolroom, you know." Hephzibah continued, "And why do you ask, child?"

Bella gave her beautiful smile, white teeth sparkling, "Well,

Miz Hephzibah, Joseph is hoping we can get married." Hephzibah gave a deep sigh and smiled in turn, "Bella, child, it is so hard to think of you all grown up now. Do you love him?"

"Oh, yes, Miz Hephzibah, I really do. And he is a grand worker, you know. When he finishes his work every day, he is never idle; he just keeps working. He's put away a neat little nest egg." Such initiative pleased Hephzibah, although it was not something she would bring up in conversation with her husband. They would not agree on the wisdom or importance of such initiative.

"Of course you have my approval, dear child. And I pray God will bless your marriage. You are special to me; you know that," and she fondly hugged the young woman.

'Rinthia and Martha were thrilled with Bella's news and made plans for special ways to help her prepare for the big day. There had ever been a close relationship between the three young women. Love was their bond, no matter that this might appear highly unusual to friends and family alike. Hephzibah had the plantation seamstress plan a lovely new dress for Bella as a wedding surprise, and Bella glowed on her big day. The wedding was planned for the Saturday of that month when Dr. Furman would be on Edisto, and there was a general air of celebration about Bleak Hall that day. Hephzibah drew Bella aside the morning of her wedding to give her a special word of blessing. She hugged the excited young bride and looking into her eyes, softly spoke, "Bella, I just wish Maum Jean were here to see you today. I have no doubt, dear child," she assured her, "that she is smiling just now and is so proud of you."

Life was never dull around Bleak Hall, and with the new year of 1811, a busy Hephzibah Townsend was soon to be even busier.

She was expecting another baby, although tiny Amarinthia was not yet five months old. This was no doubt going to be a big New Year's surprise for Daniel. Finding him in their library following family devotions that evening, Hephzibah walked over to the desk where Daniel was working on some plantation accounts and seated herself in a nearby chair. "Daniel," she began, "I have a bit of New Year's news for you if you have a moment."

Townsend sighed, leaned back in his chair and gave a wary look at his wife, no doubt expecting yet another bit of unusual news from his beloved but unpredictable spouse. "Of course, my dear," he tentatively smiled, "always more than a moment for you."

In her turn, Hephzibah gave a mischievous smile and explained, "No need to look alarmed; this is actually not a bit of news I have never before shared with you." Taking a deep breath, she finished, "Daniel, you are going to be a father yet again."

Townsend responded this time with a decided twinkle in his eye, "My dear, dear wife, let me ask you, after three little girls, beautiful little girls of course," and the twinkle grew, "I'm wondering if you might not now go back to your original pattern and give us a son this time around?" Hephzibah's fine eyes shone as she noted that certain glimmer in his eye, so reminiscent of the look that had captivated her heart as a young teenaged girl.

"I'll do my best," she responded demurely, "but we will have to wait until about August to find out for sure."

Pregnancy did not noticeably slow down Hephzibah's pace, although as the months passed she had to slow down a bit. After all, she was thirty-one years old and this was her tenth time to give birth. The Wadmalaw-Edisto Mite Society was her delight, and

she thrived on watching her fellow members resourcefully find
ways to make their contributions. They surprised themselves with
their creativity. Hephzibah and Eliza Adams had been chosen by
the society to serve as co-treasurers, and they were planning to
submit their mission offering for their first year to the Charleston
Baptist Association to report at its annual meeting. Hephzibah was
as proud of the society as she was of her own children and indeed
often felt like a fond mother, although she was by no means the
oldest in the group. News that Dr. Furman shared about William
Carey's progress in India felt like personal tidings to the women
who had developed a proprietary sense of ownership about being
part of a missions endeavor. Furman was in correspondence with
both Carey and the Baptists in England who were supporting
the work, and the fledgling society felt themselves a part of that
ministry as well. Each woman had managed to make a personal
contribution to the fund and eagerly looked forward to seeing
how much they, together, had been able to contribute during this
first year.

The mite society had gotten its start just before the birth of
Amarinthia, and as if in commemoration of that signal event, just
two days prior to Amarinthia's first birthday, Hephzibah once
more went into labor. Shortly before midnight on August 17, baby
Daniel Jenkins Townsend announced his arrival by exercising a
healthy pair of lungs. Daniel Townsend doted on his daughters,
but beamed with joy over this precious namesake, who looked
out at his new world with eyes much the same vivid shade of blue
as those of his gratified father. The tiny baby was actually named
for both his proud father and his maternal grandfather as well.

As Hephzibah cradled her sleeping baby boy in her arms, she thought of the dreams she was already forming for this beautiful child, along with her dreams for a church right here at home. It had become a calling in her heart and *surely,* the tired new mother mused, *the good Lord does have a point for me being here. Maybe this church is part of that point. I want this dream to live, just like this cherished bundle lives,* and on the thought, she fell to sleep with the hint of a smile on her face.

– Twenty –

1811-1813

LUTHER RICE COMES TO CHARLESTON

Hephzibah remembered well her papa's maxim about ways not wanting if you had the will. Well, she had plenty of will, she daily assured herself, and the ways must come from the mind God had given her. That mind was awhirl with the way the gingerbread business was developing. Nonetheless, the canny mistress of Bleak Hall was careful not to make a point of how much income the Saturday market was garnering; after all, there was no need to unnecessarily mention the subject in Daniel's presence. The whole matter was a sore spot for her dignified husband. To his mind, a wife was to be cherished and protected, not to be involved in crass commerce. Consequently, Hephzibah worked hard at preserving the appearance of a pampered and indulged wife, but it was no easy task. Her mind never slowed down.

Nor did motherhood ever seem to slow down. Hephzibah realized about the time autumn arrived that yet another child would be arriving next summer. Daniel was becoming quite accustomed to Hephzibah's announcements of impending arrivals, but he was always pleased with the news, enjoying the feeling that he was surely the fulfillment of the passage in Psalms about a man's wife like a fruitful vine and his sons like olive shoots.

Hephzibah felt that since the Charleston market on Saturday

was proving so successful, it might work to expand the amount of production — that would allow enough funds for both the mite society and the construction of a church building. And of course Bella was a huge part of the whole plan. Her baking prowess was at the heart of the enterprise. A grinning Bella was quick to let Miz Hephzibah know she was all for this new idea of expansion. It was her delight to be creative in the kitchen and at the same time know she, too, was important and necessary to God's work. Bella added some news of her own; she had a baby on the way. She informed Miz Hephzibah that Joseph couldn't seem to keep a smile off his face, he was that excited. Hephzibah automatically thought of how thrilled Maum Jean would have been with such news. That remarkable slave woman would forever be an influence on this plantation.

Hephzibah proceeded to sound Bella out about a new approach in this "missions business." Did Bella think they might cater for some special events? Bake wedding cakes? Direct receptions? Hephzibah would make the contacts and plan how to cater for weddings and special family occasions, and Bella would direct the baking. There was not a baking enterprise closer than Charleston to plan such events for the wealthy planters of Edisto. Might not this be a source of income with which to build a church?

Young Bella was a bit startled when she first heard of the idea. Wise beyond her years, she had a strong suspicion that Master Daniel wouldn't be very happy about this, but then, she thought, no doubt Miz Hephzibah could handle that right well. Bella began dreaming fanciful cakes and treats, deciding that an Edisto "event" could become the talk of the town. As the two of them talked, Hephzibah sensed that Bella, as well as her mistress, had a sense of mission about what they were doing. Who would have ever believed such affinity of hearts between mistress and slave? Surely this was a rare gift.

Hephzibah Townsend was nobody's fool, and she went about laying the foundation for her project very quietly. One evening after dinner, with just the two of them in the study, she began by assuring Daniel that she was dead serious about having a Baptist church on Edisto. Next, she explained that she had an idea that she and Bella could help out with special occasions there on Edisto, a little bit like expanding what they were already doing, and that should bring in funds to go toward building a church.

Daniel was clearly not pleased with Hephzibah's newest plans. To call him simply perturbed was an understatement. In fact, a rather lengthy "domestic discussion" ensued from Hephzibah's introduction of her new fund-raising ideas. Her husband's immediate reaction was to inquire, "Wife, have you let your brains leak out?" Townsend was frankly incensed to think of the personal embarrassment of all the other planters commenting on his lack of ability to "adequately provide" for his wife, to say nothing of being "head of the house." Their give-and-take became more than a little acrimonious, but time had taught Daniel not to allow himself to be nibbled to death by this particular duck. The disagreement ended in a stalemate, which usually indicated that Hephzibah would quietly proceed to do what she felt she needed to do.

Sure enough, within months, she, Bella, and their helpers had catered and carried out in fine fashion the wedding reception of a young planter to a beautiful young woman from a nearby plantation. The happy parents of the bride received all sorts of compliments on the event, and word began to spread. Soon, the team of Hephzibah and Bella had as much business as they could handle — nearly too much, in fact. It became popular to have a privately catered occasion, and Hephzibah rejoiced to see the funds for a Baptist church on Edisto grow apace.

When the mite society next met, the women began teasing their dear Hephzibah about being "The Gingerbread Lady." She was quick to let them know she had no right to that title. It properly belonged to Bella. The society was eagerly looking forward to their next meeting late in the summer of 1812. The Charleston Baptist Association would meet in October, and the women were going to send their first annual missions offering to the gathering.

As the ladies met at Bleak Hall that September and with Eliza Adams and Hephzibah as treasurers, each woman happily brought her contribution. Those funds had been lovingly planned and earned, and now were given with joy. Each member had been unique in what she did, finding her own creative way to contribute. Next, the treasurers began counting the money in the basket placed in the center of the beautiful dining table. The tally — $122.50! The group began to clap, and there were congratulations voiced on every front. The total exceeded all their expectations. It was just too bad that none of them could attend the associational meeting in October at the High Hills.

However, Hephzibah was pleased to explain to the group that her good friend, Rachel Furman Baker, now lived in Sumter and would be able to attend the sessions. And of course, their dear Dr.

Furman, the association's president, would himself present their mite society offering to the assembled body.

Accordingly, when the group next met in November, Hephzibah passed on Rachel's report, telling how Dr. Furman had presented their offering as he told the association about the formation of this unique mite society. Rachel further reported that the Wadmalaw-Edisto Female Mite Society offering was the largest single missions offering in all the association. Hephzibah read aloud, "It was reported at annual meeting, received by the hands of the president, 122 dollars, 50 cents transmitted to him by Mrs. Eliza A. Adams and Mrs. Hephzibah Townsend, Treasurers of the Wadmalaw and Edisto Female Mite Society, in aid of the Missionary Fund," whereupon the ladies broke into spontaneous applause. It had been a wonderful first year, and none was prouder than their oldest member, Abby Mikell, frail though she was.

In fact, Hephzibah was growing quite concerned about her beloved Aunt Abby, who was noticeably failing. Late in November, Hephzibah received a note from Cousin Joseph saying his mama was getting very weak; could Hephzibah come? Within two hours, Hephzibah was at her aunt's side. Abby had been hit by dysentery and, already debilitated with painful arthritis, could not seem to bounce back. She wasn't in severe pain, but seemed to realize that her days were numbered. The two women, old and young, had a special bond that went far beyond kinship and common interests. Aunt Abby had been much of a mother figure in Hephzibah Townsend's life, and the two women spent the day together. They reminisced over times gone by, and Hephzibah found ways to express her heart's gratitude to her beloved Abby. The following

Saturday, December 5, Aunt Abby breathed her last, surrounded by her cherished son, her grandchildren and Hephzibah Jenkins Townsend, the loved daughter she had never had.

Bella was sparkling these days, busy with all her responsibilities, happy in her new home and expecting her first baby. 'Rinthia was beaming herself about this time, and as Hephzibah called it, smelling of April and May. 'Rinthia's young man, William Wilkinson, had asked for her hand in marriage, and Daniel, standing in place of her father, gladly gave his consent. Wilkinson was a strong Christian with a good business head on him; furthermore, he palpably adored 'Rinthia, and Hephzibah applauded him for his great good taste.

The wedding took place in Charleston on March 23, and to no one's surprise, the wedding breakfast was given by Hephzibah Townsend and attended by a throng of relatives and friends both from Edisto and Charleston. The newlyweds had decided to begin their lives together in a little house on the property willed to Amarinthia by her father, with plans to build their own home nearby as soon as they could. Hephzibah already missed having her beloved sister's presence at Bleak Hall, but 'Rinthia remained very much a part of the society and stayed closely involved in helping her sister plan for an Edisto Baptist church.

As coincidence would have it, Bella gave birth to her first child and Hephzibah to her eleventh within a month of each other. Bella's little Lewis was born in May and the plantation servants were excited about the baby. Bella was a favorite in the slave community, and a tight-knit one it was. Bleak Hall slaves carried on many of the Gullah traditions from the old country along with a unique language of their own developed from the language of their ancestry, charmingly mixed with English, nearly incomprehensible to someone hearing it for the first time. Like Bella, her son Lewis would likely grow up speaking Gullah along with low-country English.

Then on June 22, young William Adams Townsend announced his arrival, and Daniel and Hephzibah joked that they were now on a run of male children. John Ferrars was a teenager and it would not be long until he went away to college; he was especially strong in the classics but enjoyed history as well. All the children were thriving, with Mary Frampton and Martha Susan happily learning to read and cipher, and Amarinthia and little Daniel Jenkins, the young ones, toddling around everywhere.

William's doting mother was not only busy with her newborn and her flourishing business, but was also laying the groundwork for the eventual construction of a Baptist church. Even as Hephzibah added funds slowly but surely through the market sales and weddings and events that she and Bella were catering, she went to work on securing use of the land where the 1700s Baptist church had stood. Hephzibah enjoyed a close relationship with the Episcopal congregation since childhood, when she had frequently attended services there with her dear papa. As a result, there was a willingness among current leaders at Trinity Church to allow Hephzibah Townsend to use the property that they had been renting for building a Baptist church right where one had stood a century earlier. After all, that was part of the legal conditions spelled out as to how the land could be used.

One of the stipulations was that a church had to be successfully established within ten years in order for the property to be used by the Baptists. In the back of Hephzibah's mind, she sensed that the brethren in leadership at Trinity likely had an idea that she might not be able to get the job done in that period of time. After all, it would need to be an established church with a minister and a congregation. Otherwise, the land would revert back to the use of the Episcopalians. The Episcopalians might harbor such thoughts, but not Hephzibah Jenkins Townsend. She had come to think of this task as a mission given her by the Lord Himself.

For his part, Pastor Furman encouraged and assisted Hephzibah in every way he could. Along with her, he yearned to see an active Baptist witness on the beautiful little island, a place to carry on the legacy of those early Baptist leaders who had worshipped there. Due to the bequest from the pioneer Ephraim Mikell, the Euhaw Baptist congregation — descendants of the original church — were receiving rent monies from the land. Furman urged the congregation, however, to assign Mrs. Townsend use of the property for the purpose of constructing a church on the land.

In typical nineteenth-century fashion, Furman addressed his correspondence to Hephzibah through her husband, and the good Presbyterian elder was chivalrous enough to support his wife in her efforts, reluctant as he was for her to do any such unfeminine thing as lead out in establishing a church. In Townsend's mind he was shaking his head no, but outwardly he was standing as supportive husband for his forceful wife, no matter that he thought it a waste of her time and energy and certainly not her place as a woman. Daniel Townsend had never before in his fifty-some years encountered a woman with so much determination and grit, a woman who looked every bit the part of a lady, but somehow continued to assert herself in a way he could only deplore. Nonetheless, he unwaveringly loved her and secretly admired the depth of her determination. For her part, Hephzibah usually had the great good sense to know when to push ahead and when to acquiesce on a point that was not vital. In sixteen years of marriage, she had learned some things about thrust and parry and what battles were worth her time and energy. No fool she, this chatelaine of Bleak Hall.

Then about the time little William was four months old, Dr. Furman announced momentous news. Rev. Luther Rice, that dynamic young man who had sailed as one of the first foreign missionaries just the year before, was coming to First Baptist Charleston. When Hephzibah heard the news, she determined to be in Charleston that weekend. Mr. Rice had gone to the Far East the winter of 1812, within weeks of the sailing of Ann and Adoniram Judson. Rice's health failed, however, and he came close to death with liver disease. Forced to return to America to spare his life, he took up the task of telling the story of the Judsons and the urgent need for Baptists to organize to support them. Hephzibah listened with wide eyes and fast-beating heart as Rice told how he and the Judsons, waiting in India to find a country in which to serve, had been convinced of their need to be immersed. So it was that the Judsons and Rice were baptized at the Lal Bazaar Church in Calcutta, and now here they were, Baptists, but with no supporting body, for Baptists in America had not organized as a denomination.

Now here in Charleston was Luther Rice — tall, handsome, committed, a compelling speaker, traveling from Massachusetts to South Carolina and rallying Baptists, encouraging them to organize and support the Judsons, their first missionaries. Ann and Adoniram were already laboring away in heathen Burmah, but needing prayer and funds from home in order to share the gospel message. Hephzibah was captivated. These were American missionaries. These were Baptists and they needed support!

Following the morning service that crisp November Sunday, Richard Furman had the honor of introducing Luther Rice to Mrs. Townsend, organizer of the one and only mite society in the South, a group willing and eager to give just such support as Mr. Rice was pleading for. An instant friendship was forged that morning. These were kindred spirits with kindred callings. Hephzibah promised Mr. Rice that as soon as Baptists organized, he could count on their little society to do their utmost to support the Judsons. She assured him she could scarcely wait to return to Edisto and report to the society about what God was doing in faraway Burmah. This news from Luther Rice was like an affirmation to Hephzibah Townsend — the realization that God was at work all around the world and that a small group of dedicated ladies on a tiny and obscure low-country island might actually be able to make an eternal difference.

MINUTES OF THE GENERAL COMMITTEE.

1. The following delegates appeared—Furman, Roberts, Nixon, Paulling, Tucker, Evans, Huggins, and Good.

2. Elected officers, Richard Furman President, David Adams Treasurer, John M. Roberts Secretary, James Harper and Isaac Gill Assistants.

3. Received, by the hands of the President, 122 dollars. 50 cents, transmitted to him by Mrs. Eliza A. Adams and Mrs. Hephzibah Townsend, Treasurers of the Wadmalaw and Edisto Female Mite Society, in aid of the Missionary Fund.

Agreed that the thanks of this body be given to those Ladies, and the society for their pious liberality.

4. Mr. Allan Sweat appeared as a candidate for the Churches' bounty, with a Recommendation from the Church at Pipe Creek; underwent examination, and was approved. Whereupon, agreed, that as soon as the state of the fund will admit of it, he shall be placed on the churches' bounty.

5. Agreed that the special committee continue to exercise the powers of the general committee, in things necessary, during the recess of this body.

6. Took an account of the contributions, and state of the fund, as exhibited below.

	Education Fund.		*Missionary Fund.*	
Charleston, contrib.	$194		$ 84	87½
High Hills Santee,	25		25	
Congaree,	2		5	
Amelia Township,	5		10	
Welsh Neck,	24	Wadmal. & Edis. Mite Soc.	122	50
Columbia,	18 37½			
Beulah,	11	Expenditure,	247	37½
Three Creeks,	13	Paid to Missi. $121 43½		
		do. School Mas. 90 94 } 247 37½		
Charleston collection rec'd by late Treas. deducted, }	292 37½ 194	do. Educa. Fund, $5		
	98 37½	Remains due Mr. Lewis the School Master, }	$150	6
	or £ 22 19 1			
Specialties in hands of President	929 3 4			
Cash in hands of do.	27 4 11			
Cash repaid from Miss. Funds,	8 3 4			
Cash in hands of late T's Exec.	228 12 4			

£1216 3 0

The Expenditures, as appears by receipted vouchers, have this Year amounted to £167 15 4.

Record from Charleston Baptist Association minutes, October 1812, showing the initial contribution of the Wadmalaw-Edisto Female Mite Society. (Courtesy Historical Services, South Carolina Baptist Convention.)

~ Twenty-One ~

1814-1816
A DENOMINATION IS BORN

Exciting news came from Charleston in May of 1814. Dr. Furman was on an extended trip to Philadelphia to attend the first official gathering of Baptists from across the country. Its purpose was to organize in order to support missions; Luther Rice had done his work well, and there was a general air of excitement and anticipation as delegates from various states gathered in the City of Brotherly Love. On May 14, a Baptist denomination was birthed in America. Its long name was a mind boggler: The General Baptist Missionary Convention of the Baptist Denomination in the United States of America for Foreign Missions. Thankfully, it was going to simply be called The Triennial Convention. That was a lot easier to handle.

Hephzibah was thrilled to learn that not only had her beloved pastor given the keynote message, but Richard Furman was also elected the convention's first president. The mite society on Edisto was further elated to learn that their contribution of forty-four dollars, delivered in person by Dr. Furman, was the largest single offering given by any society. This meant that women in the low country were helping further the gospel in faraway Burmah; the news was both exciting and invigorating.

On the home front, Hephzibah's family remained busy.

'Rinthia and William were living in a small house on property Daniel Jenkins had willed his daughter. The young couple planned to build a new plantation house as soon as possible. And sister Martha finally said yes to young Richard LaRoche. For the wedding day, Hephzibah and Bella planned a beautiful reception in honor of the occasion.

In all honesty, the baking business was growing apace and often the days just seemed to run out of enough hours. The venture had exceeded Hephzibah's expectations and she was happily surprised. Moreover, the mistress of Bleak Hall seemed to have developed the ability to appear serene in the midst of massive responsibilities. Truthfully, her dependency upon the Heavenly Father was growing apace as well. She often came to the end of a day that had been far too harried and filled with one problem after another, and realize all afresh her reliance on the guidance of the Holy Spirit. And in those quiet moments, she again reflected that she was simply a sinner saved by grace, and one who had surely been given a task to do.

Charleston trips were a time to break from routine and refresh her spirit, as well as an opportunity to conduct business by getting supplies and making contacts for the work she was expanding. Increasingly, Hephzibah gave thanks for the acumen as well as the dedication of a young slave woman. What would she ever do without Bella? Only twenty-two now, Bella was mature far beyond her years, and she was a force among the Bleak Hall slave community. She and her Joseph had their cabin near the big house. When Miz Townsend needed something done, she only had to mention it to Bella and the task would be done. Bella's young Lewis was a winsome child, and he and little William were often seen around the grounds together, always under the watchful eye of Maum Nancy.

Hephzibah, now a venerable thirty-four, was the mother of six living children. The baby William was scarcely a year old and John Ferrars was going off to college. How could it be? She asked herself that age-old question: Where has the time gone? However, Hephzibah was a bit concerned about her eldest, John. He was very much a boy, reveling in sport, whether shooting or riding.

What most concerned his mother, however, was his attitude. To her observant eyes, she saw in him a sense of superiority that she found disquieting, and often he made a remark or acted in a way that revealed a sense of entitlement. She mused that all too often, when privilege was in place, a sense of privilege so often seemed to follow. John had certainly not learned that feeling of entitlement at his mother's knee. So many times Hephzibah would tell her children about the gift of life given her by Maum Jean and Jack, who had risked their own lives to save hers. These were her people. It was an oft-repeated story each Townsend child heard.

On the other hand, John was faithful in attendance at the Presbyterian church, worshipping regularly with his father. It did disturb Hephzibah that the family normally did not worship together since she attended services in Charleston and not with Daniel. However, her sense of what was right for her was too strong to allow her to deny her conviction that she was a Baptist at heart and a Baptist she would remain. She did make sure that on special occasions she went with Daniel and John to the Edisto Presbyterian church.

It was John's attitude toward the servants that struck a note of uneasiness in Hephzibah. She wished he had known Maum Jean and could appreciate the need for dignity of those who were enslaved. His attitude smacked of arrogance, and this troubled her. For years she repeated to John the story of her miraculous survival as a baby and how Maum Jean and Jack were the reason that she lived. These were her people, she explained over and over. Nonetheless, her eldest son seemed to look on it as simply a story. It did not appear to impact him personally or to affect his attitude of superiority. She grieved that John did not seem to show respect to the servants. On the other hand, he never failed to accord respect and affection to his mother, and she did appreciate that. However, that just wasn't enough, for she feared this arrogant attitude affected his outlook on life.

For his part, Daniel seemed to think it perfectly fine that their son would be going to South Carolina College and taking his body servant, Daddy Sam, to wait on him. Hephzibah personally found this both indulgent and self-serving, no matter that many of John's young planter classmates would be doing the same thing. Nevertheless, John's mother decided to keep her tongue between her teeth on this one; she was slowly developing the ability to choose her battles. The college was some 130 miles from Edisto, but their plans were for John to transfer to Princeton in a year or so, and that would certainly be much farther away.

A time or so each year, the mistress of Bleak Hall managed to get in a visit with Rachel Baker when both of them were in Charleston. Her longtime friend would come to visit her Furman family whenever she had a chance. The distance between Sumter and Charleston made those chances infrequent. Hephzibah relished these infrequent cozes with Rachel. This oldest daughter of Richard Furman had only one son during the first decade of her marriage, but three years ago another boy had been born, and then last year, at long last, she gave birth to a little girl. All these years, Rachel marveled at the size of Hephzibah's family, gently teasing her about having more to do than a mortal could handle.

Another tie Hephzibah maintained with her youth was an occasional opportunity to visit with Eliza Pinckney when she went to Charleston. Her old friend was now Eliza Izard, having married the naval hero of Tripoli, Ralph Lelancy Izard. Hephzibah might be more than busy, but she had never lost her early fascination with the mechanics of government and the intriguing stories of colonial derring-do. By dint of the Pinckney family's long history of leadership in the early foundations of America's government, and now her husband's personal involvement in military leadership, Eliza was always abreast of what was going on in South Carolina politics, as well as in Washington. Hephzibah perpetually had a store of questions to run by her old friend when they had a chance to get together. On the other hand, Eliza did not have children of her own and was eager to hear accounts of Hephzibah's brood, all six of them.

Their number was soon to grow, for in April of 1815, Benjamin Joseph Townsend joined the family, the third straight son after the birth of three daughters. Young Daniel was four now, and William already two. That same November, 'Rinthia's first child was born and named Martha for both her aunt and her grandmother.

The mite society tried to meet every other month, and the

women eagerly looked forward to any news Dr. Furman could give them about the work of the Judsons in Burmah. It took many months for letters to travel across the Pacific, and any news was highly anticipated. Society members had grown quite adept at finding ways to raise funds. For her part, Hephzibah was most pleased to check her accounting books at the end of each month and see how the nest egg for constructing a church was also slowly but steadily accumulating.

In contemplating the construction and founding of a church, Hephzibah Townsend was well aware of the challenges she confronted. There were no Baptist men on Edisto who seemed to sense the importance of having a Baptist presence on the island once more. After all, Edisto was primarily a place dominated by what some might call a planter aristocracy, and Baptists were noted for being less elitist than the Presbyterians or Episcopalians. On the other hand, the Baptists and Methodists were considered less class-conscious and more clearly concerned about the soul condition of slaves.

No fool, Hephzibah Townsend; it was a man's world in which they lived, and she would of necessity have to live in the system as it was. She couldn't change it, but she could function within it, using the mind the good Lord gave her and figuring out ways to work within the current scheme of things. At least, when it came to pious endeavors, a woman taking a bit of initiative was viewed as slightly more palatable among the planter class. Not for nothing had Hephzibah Jenkins Townsend been developing that adage Papa had impressed upon his young daughter: For he who wills, ways are not wanting.

She had learned well the lesson of not depending on her spouse to help her with benevolent giving. However, Mrs. Townsend was fast becoming adept at circumventing the system when necessary. If nothing else, it was clear that Daniel believed a true gentleman should be chivalrous, and therefore he had in several instances defended his wife, at least in public; this was something she was coming to rely on. However much they might disagree and however angry he might become at some of what he considered her foolhardy actions, he nevertheless unfailingly stood by her in the eyes of the world. The instinctive sense Hephzibah had that Daniel would never leave her defenseless was like a bulwark of encouragement. Although he might often privately despair of her "wild notions," he invariably stood with her in public. Hephzibah concluded that she was not consciously manipulating her husband; she was simply using the prevailing system to accomplish what her heart told her was the right thing to do. If a lady was able to manage her plantation through her men, why not manage a church that way as well? It was something to ponder. Sometimes the name of the game could be negotiation, and Hephzibah would negotiate when necessary. Through the years, she honed well the skill to sometimes bend but never break.

Early in 1816, Hephzibah read the telltale signs clearly: She was expecting yet again. At thirty-six years old, a lesser woman might have found that daunting. Not so Hephzibah Townsend. This was her thirteenth pregnancy. At least she knew what to expect. Her body was beginning to show a bit of wear, however, and she discovered that she tired more easily and had to pace herself more carefully. Daniel was shaking his head and grinning at the idea of yet another child. This baby was due in October, but sorrow was to engulf the Townsend household before that time, for in April little William, not yet three years old, contracted a lung infection and not even the best efforts of the doctors could spare his life.

The composure that the grieving mother seemed to wear so easily was actually a garment she had put on with hard discipline. Again, she felt the echo of a distant pain as she recalled those shattering days after the grievous loss of so many in such a short time some twelve years earlier. Hephzibah would cup her hands protectively around her swelling abdomen and plead with God to protect this new life growing in her. How could she deal with so much sorrow? Practice certainly didn't lessen the pain. Another little grave now stood next to those of other beloved ones now forever gone. Her greatest comfort was the sure knowledge that in heaven they would once more be together.

With her usual quiet dignity, Hephzibah maintained an iron discipline over herself; through sheer force of will, her daily work and involvement did not suffer. Only she knew that many a night she closed her eyes and wished that when she woke again she would find it all to be a nightmare, something chased away by the sunlight streaming in her bedroom window. But morning would come and the grief remained. It was real, and she would simply have to live with the aching loss that never quite went away.

Summer came and went, and October brought in autumn and the time for yet another new baby in the house. October 11, 1816, and tiny Sarah Calder Townsend had her first look at the world; she looked amazingly like big sister Mary Frampton, who at age twelve was on the threshold of womanhood herself. Mary doted on her tiny look-alike, and the children could hardly wait for Baby to get big enough to play and coo and babble. Hephzibah hardly missed a beat, and her days were busy from the moment she arose until she tiredly sank into her feather mattress each night, always weary but invariably with her mind still going strong.

Hephzibah could not recall a time in her married life when she had passed any long stretch of time without some crisis, small or large. Just as she started thinking that everything was moving along smoothly, as sure as the sun rises in the morning, something occurred to ripple the waters of tranquility. It did yet again, and this conflict was one that Hephzibah had realized, in the back reaches of her mind, would inevitably one day crop up. Daniel was fifty-seven years old now. Her own papa had died when just fifty. Daniel had been hinting about wanting to make his will. One never knows, he suggested. Better be prepared.

Hephzibah foresaw trouble ahead. A body could feel it in the bones. She knew all too well what Daniel felt about the old English law of primogeniture, with all the inheritance going to an oldest son. That law was diametrically opposed to her own sentiments. Troubles were bound to be just around the corner, and she steeled herself for the dissension that seemed inevitable. Here was a coming battle, one she would not be able to avoid. She began praying specifically for wisdom and strength of mind and heart. Be that as it may, now was no time to be distracted by something over which she had no control. There was a church to be founded, and with God as her Polar Star she was intent upon accomplishing this task.

~ Twenty-Two ~

1817-1819

A CHURCH IS REBORN

Hephzibah was growing increasingly excited about construction on the church actually starting. Never mind that the land disputes continued, with the state legislature overturning the decision they made in 1808. Euhaw Baptist Church was reasserting its claim to the land as opposed to the Episcopalians, but Hephzibah had decided to waste no time on legal maneuverings and instead to quietly proceed with building. How grateful she was for the fine carpenters on the Townsend plantation, and one of the best was Bella's Joseph. Joseph had been apprenticed out to a skilled carpenter as a young boy and his skills were impressive. Furthermore, he was one of Miz Hephzibah Jenkins's family servants and felt a deep loyalty toward her. She in turn decided to use Joseph to head up the building project, asking him to assemble a crew to see to the construction of a simple but sturdy structure for the proposed Baptist church. Pastor Furman enlisted men in the Charleston church to provide the building plans, and Joseph would follow those drawings.

Hephzibah went about her preparations unobtrusively, arranging for Joseph and his crew to spend a brief time each evening after their regular duties to begin construction. Funds were in hand, and it appeared to Mrs. Townsend, the astute businesswoman, that it was going to take about $2,000 in hard cash to build the structure. In the back of her mind, she could envision the balcony — but her personal intention was that the gallery would not be for slaves, rather that worshippers at Edisto Baptist could sit where they pleased. Knowing the idea would no doubt be controversial, she discussed it only with 'Rinthia, this sister who was much more dear than just a sister. God being her helper, this congregation would be one where everyone would know they were equal in the eyes of their Maker.

Daniel grumbled a bit about "our workers spending evenings working on something unnecessary," but being preoccupied with all his own responsibilities, he did not keep close tabs on what was going on with construction. Hephzibah certainly did not discuss progress on the building with him, knowing all too well his feelings about the matter.

Occasionally, Townsend would let drop a cynical remark about there being no need to "have a church for slaves." Hephzibah found this offensive, realizing this was one of the points on which she and Daniel were never likely to agree. She had discovered that her best response to such provocative statements was no response at all. She was also keenly aware that the slave population in the low country had grown dramatically, especially since Sea Island Cotton had become so highly prized and was such a labor-intensive industry. Slaves now far outnumbered the white population of Edisto and these folk needed spiritual nourishment just as did their white masters. They were equally God's children; why couldn't Daniel acknowledge that? In the back of her mind, she could hear Maum Jean's dear old voice urging her on with a

"That's right, honey chile."

It was during this time that John Ferrars became seriously ill. His faithful body servant, Daddy Sam, managed to get him home from college, and the doctor diagnosed the dreaded yellow fever. For days they despaired for his life, but judicious use of calomel and castor oil, along with medicinal salts, proved the turning point — and John Ferrars, young and healthy when struck, slowly began to recover. Several months later, he was able to leave for Princeton University, and until his graduation several years later seldom had an opportunity to get back to Edisto.

On her frequent trips to Charleston following her son's illness, Hephzibah kept Dr. Furman abreast of progress on the church building. On the Saturdays when Furman could make it to Edisto for services, he viewed the construction project with great interest. In the spring of 1818, Hephzibah began making nearly daily visits to the site as the building neared completion. She met several times with Richard Furman to plan the opening service. 'Rinthia joined her sister in getting the word of the opening service out to the planters of Edisto. Several who had Baptist forebears showed much interest and were planning to come, as were a number who wanted to attend out of simple curiosity. The grapevine on the slave network was highly efficient as well, and the word spread: "Miz Hephzibah's church is about ready, and we are welcome."

The long-anticipated rebirth of Edisto Baptist Church finally arrived on May 23, and the brand new sanctuary was full, both on the main floor as well as in the balcony. Most of the slaves were too hesitant to sit on the ground floor, although a few bolder ones lingered at the back. Dr. Richard Furman, the leading Baptist minister of his day, brought the opening message, and there sat Hephzibah Jenkins Townsend, feeling like her heart would burst with joy. This was surely an answer to prayer. Realizing that most of the people there had come out of curiosity, Hephzibah nonetheless prayed that God would build up His church in this place with those He had in mind. Hephzibah was disappointed that Daniel had not come to this opening service, although not surprised. 'Rinthia's William was there with them, however, beaming over this beginning. A member of First Baptist Charleston himself, he had offered his wife and sister-in-law encouragement all along. Hephzibah's sister Martha was also there for the big day, as were Hephzibah's own Mary and Susan. Young teenagers now, the girls were bright-eyed and excited to be at the inaugural service. Very much their mother's daughters, they, too, had "Baptist leanings."

Hephzibah looked around the sanctuary and noticed members of the Wadmalaw-Edisto Mite Society seated in several of the pews. As Dr. Furman rose to preach, those same women exchanged speaking looks of joy and anticipation. They had a church now as well as their society, and gave thanks to God. As Furman talked of the heritage that led to the rebirth of Edisto Baptist, Hephzibah thought back to Dr. Screven preaching here a hundred years earlier. Then her mind moved to her ancestors who had been part of that beginning, and thanked God that she could follow in their train.

Hephzibah had no doubt that the situation with slaves in the membership was certainly going to be a ticklish one. Although a few servants attended services at Daniel's Presbyterian church and at Trinity Episcopal, it was rather like an afterthought to the planters; certainly slaves did not feel part of the church life in those congregations. Hephzibah Townsend prayed that it would be different here at Edisto Baptist. She foresaw nothing easy in getting to that point, but then she could hear the echo of Papa's voice so long ago, "Child, nothing really important is ever easy to come by. You have to work at it." His daughter had heeded that maxim; its results were clearly defined in the force of character she exhibited. Everyone who came to Edisto Baptist would be an important part of this fellowship, and all of them respected as part of the body of Christ. This was Hephzibah Townsend's heartfelt wish.

The mite society would be an integral part of the church, although a number of its members belonged to other denominations. All of them looked forward to society meetings when new editions of *Missionary Intelligencer* arrived. Nearly every issue contained a letter from Ann and Adoniram Judson, and the society went from month to month wondering what news they would next hear from exotic Burmah. The conditions in which this couple lived in the Far East were difficult to even imagine for women living in comfortable America. When word finally came of the first Burmese convert in 1819, members of the Edisto Mite Society were overjoyed. Hephzibah's oldest girls, Mary and Susan were very much a part of the group, and at fourteen and fifteen were already becoming quite knowledgeable about early missions endeavors.

Meanwhile, 'Rinthia and William were working on a different structure — their own plantation home. When the work was completed, an excited 'Rinthia dubbed it The Summit, declaring it to be the summit of her dreams of a house. The Wilkinsons, along with their three little ones, moved into The Summit in 1819.

Just about the time Edisto Baptist Church had its rebirth, one of the most traumatic periods in Hephzibah's already harried life was looming on the horizon. Daniel's hints of getting ready to write his will had now come to the point of him actually sitting down to formulate his plans. Townsend kept all the details to himself, clearly reluctant to discuss them with Hephzibah, knowing as he did that the two of them took absolutely polarized views on the proposed will. For some reason, Townsend remained enamored of the British idea of primogeniture, which provided that all the land holdings would automatically go to the eldest son.

Had there been just one child, this would have presented no problems. That was not the case; there were seven children, and Daniel's wife could see nothing fair about leaving out the other six. It was especially galling to think of Daniel planning in his will to allocate all the property to just their eldest son, especially considering that the land and inheritance she had brought to the marriage far exceeded Daniel's own holdings. She could only see trouble ahead, for indeed her sense of justice was too deeply ingrained to be able to accept the concept of primogeniture. That could not be fair.

All too soon for Hephzibah the confrontation came. Daniel had appeared to be in ill humor much of the time of late; something was clearly gnawing at him. Hephzibah had been married to the man for more than twenty years; she could read the signs. Sure enough, one evening after the children had gone to bed, Daniel asked his wife to come into the study with him. A worm of apprehension began to gnaw at her stomach. Here it was. Hephzibah steeled herself for what she expected to be a difficult discussion, one fraught with strong feelings on both sides. Her back straightened and she took a deep breath, dreading what was just ahead.

At first Daniel seemed unable to do any more than clear his throat and fiddle around with the pens and sheets of paper on his desk. Then he launched into his plans. It was his feeling, he assured her, that he needed to make sure their wealth remained intact and therefore he was going to will all their land and holdings to John Ferrars as the eldest son. Before Hephzibah could even make a rejoinder, he began enumerating his reasons; within minutes, he didn't need any wind from someone else to fill his sails. He was going full force, with no intention of listening to any comments other than his own.

When Daniel finally had to pause for breath and Hephzibah had a chance to express herself, matters became increasingly tense. "Daniel," she spoke as calmly as her agitated emotions would allow, "did you even stop to consider that well over half the land and holdings we have are those I brought to our marriage?" Daniel opened his mouth to retort, but Hephzibah gave him no opportunity, "Don't tell me the law states that a husband controls the property. I am no slow wit," and by now her magnificent dark eyes were flashing with emotion. "That is a law I would reshape if I could. I know the law; I also know what is just. This is not just. Can you honestly tell me you think it is?" she asked him. Of course he could, and proceeded to inform her that brilliant minds in legislatures had formed those policies for the common

good and how could she, a mere woman, have a better understanding than those learned men as to what was best? Townsend
then proceeded to give his wife a lecture that would have taken
the varnish off the family silver.

When he paused for breath, Hephzibah attempted reasoning
with him. "How," she asked him, "can you possibly think it fair
that our oldest son, whom of course we both love, should inherit
all these thousands of acres, and our six other children receive
none? Daniel," she continued before he could open his mouth to
rebut her question, "do you remember what you said to me more
than two decades ago, back when we were courting? I clearly
recall," and here she paused, and her voice caught in her throat,
"you telling me that one of the things you most admired about me
was my sense of justice. Well, husband, my sense of justice clearly
tells me that what you plan to do is neither right nor just." By
this point, she was rapidly descending into that state of gloriously
unselfconscious indignation where one does not in the least care
what one says so long as one can score a point by saying it.

Upon which, Daniel threw a promising faggot upon the
smoldering fire of their altercation by informing his wife, that
in the end, it didn't matter what she thought; he was the head
of the house and his decision was final. Hephzibah's composure,
which she seemed to wear so easily, was actually no more than a
garment put on with hard discipline. She didn't bother to reach
up to wipe away a tear — that would mean acknowledging its
presence. Those fine dark eyes looked for the longest time into
her husband's resentful blue ones. The quiet dignity that seemed
to suddenly wrap around her like a cloak was almost palpable to

Daniel Townsend. He had learned the hard way that sometimes when Hephzibah was at her quietest, a situation might be at its most dangerous.

The scene ended like a never-to-be-finished book slamming shut, as Hephzibah wheeled around and headed to the door. Standing at the threshold, she paused and looked back at Daniel still standing there by his desk. "Never before in our many years, Daniel, have I felt that you have completely disregarded my opinion and failed to respect me." Hephzibah gave him one last look. "Husband," she concluded, "I will do what I must do," then quietly and with deliberate finality closed the door behind her.

Edisto Island Baptist Church, founded by Hephzibah Jenkins Townsend in 1818.

Historical marker honoring Hephzibah Jenkins Townsend, located in front of Edisto Island Baptist Church.

~ Twenty-Three ~

1820-1823

SHARGOULD

Hephzibah entered her bedroom and immediately closed the door behind her. She could scarcely give her feelings a name. She was hurt. She was close to despair. Daniel was completely intransigent, clearly having determined that his way was the right way and so be it. What possible choices did she have? Simply acquiesce? Forget her principles of fairness and justice? The vagrant thoughts lingered no more than a moment in her mind and were dismissed. A weary Hephzibah tilted her head on that slender neck, first to one side, then the other, half closing her eyes as she did so, and breathing deeply as if to release an inner tension.

There came to her confused and weary mind a clear realization. She recognized life for what it was — a gift. As long as this gift remained in her keeping, she would be a worthy steward of God's manifold blessings. Clearly, privilege brings responsibility, and the Lord daily touched her life with so much privilege. She must be worthy in how she used what He had blessed her with. Taking a deep breath, Hephzibah resolved to sift through the shattered pieces of their confrontation and pray for wisdom as to what to do next. Accepting the unacceptable was not an option. She gave a rueful inward grin as she reflected that her character over these years had rather boiled down to a good strong broth. Now was the time for action.

The atmosphere around Bleak Hall was more than bleak those early days of January in 1820. Children and servants alike looked about with anxious eyes, noting the chilly and formal courtesy with which the master and mistress treated each other. One could almost see the thin sheet of ice coating the hallways, brittle enough on which to slip and fall if one wasn't careful. Daniel went about his myriad tasks, far more taciturn than usual, and staying out around the plantation much longer than was his usual habit.

Two evenings later, Hephzibah paid a visit to Bella and Joseph's small cabin, playing a few moments with little Lewis, a bright-eyed engaging little scamp of a fellow, and then she got down to business. Enlisting Joseph's help, Hephzibah requested that a work crew be assembled to spend time each evening over at Shargould constructing a snug but comfortable house. Bella had a fair idea of what might be taking place, but knew to ask no questions. She and Joseph would literally have been willing to sacrifice themselves for their Miz Hephzibah, so deep was both their love and respect for this one who cherished them in return.

In his usual efficient way, Joseph went to work with a will, and within days the tabby foundation of a house could be seen taking shape just adjacent to the tabby ovens where the baking industry took place every weekday. Daniel no doubt realized some construction work was going on, but thinking it had to do with Hephzibah's foolish "mission business," remained aloof. That suited Hephzibah perfectly. At this point, "least said, soonest mended."

The timing could not have been worse, considering the icy atmosphere around Bleak Hall. *Dear Lord,* Hephzibah groaned in dismay, *what terrible timing this is — expecting yet another child!* Surely not now. She was forty years old, and these last weeks she had felt every one of those years. Here her eldest was, already a college graduate and studying law in Charleston, and his mother was expecting still another little one. In fact, Daniel had taken a portion of the property on Wadmalaw Island and given it to John Ferrars so that he would be eligible to be elected to the state legislature as soon as he was twenty-one. John had decided to stop the study of law and devote himself to running the family holdings on Wadmalaw Island.

This new one would be Hephzibah's fourteenth child, and it grieved her to think of a babe entering a home with so much discord. None of this conflict was easy on their children. Mary and Susan were both very responsible teenagers and old enough to realize that something was sorely amiss at Bleak Hall. Amarinthia was a bright ten-year-old, the winsome young Daniel nine. Benjamin was five, and already reading everything he could find at hand, and Sarah was a clever little four-year-old sprite. Hephzibah was deeply concerned about how the effects of her decision were going to impact the children and prayed earnestly for wisdom as she proceeded.

Not a word of her impending move did Hephzibah verbalize. She had stoically told Daniel about the baby due in August but not of her immediate plans. Within two months, the structure built on nearby Shargould was completed. Hephzibah gathered together necessary furniture and supplies and began furnishing the new house. One evening after dinner, Daniel, with exaggerated politeness, requested that she come to the office. Steeling her back, Hephzibah complied. "Madam Wife," he addressed her as soon as she entered the study, "I see a house standing at Shargould. I went there this afternoon to see it. Can you explain this to me?" he finished in steely tones.

"Certainly," she responded, "I can do that. Husband," she inhaled deeply, "I am moving to Shargould. I cannot in integrity remain here at Bleak Hall after the decision you made concerning our legacy." Daniel drew a breath to interrupt, whereupon Hephzibah raised an admonitory finger and gave him no time to get started, "I am not making a public display. I am still your wife and I am loyal. But as long as we are so diametrically opposed about how to will our property, I cannot in good conscience remain under this roof, on this land which was bequeathed me by my beloved mother." Pausing to catch a breath and control her agitated breathing, she proceeded, "I will continue to serve as mistress here and do my duty. Do not fear I will shirk it. Nor will I fail to honor you as my husband," and again she stopped to calm her racing heart. "I will continue to be at Bleak Hall with the children for our family evening meal, but I will be living at Shargould. You must see, Daniel," and here she could not keep her eyes from flashing, "I will not live under this roof under our present conditions."

It was seldom that Daniel Townsend found himself without words. Now was one of those rare moments. Never in all their twenty-plus years of marriage had he been so taken by surprise. Townsend was well over sixty years old now, and this was clearly a shock; it was going to take him some time to adjust.

By April, Hephzibah had moved into the Shargould house, far smaller than the magnificent Bleak Hall, but very livable. The children adjusted as children do, with great ease, because their mother was so matter of fact about their new situation. Mary and Susan were excited, because very soon now they were going to be moving to Charleston to attend finishing school. Both girls were on tiptoe with anticipation; Charleston was one of their favorite spots and they were feeling very grownup. Furthermore, they knew that two of Pastor Furman's daughters would be at their school, and Susan and Maria were just about their same age. It would be like going to school with longtime friends.

Tiny Theodora Elizabeth Townsend made her appearance on August 7, 1820, the only one of Hephzibah's babies not born at Bleak Hall. Daniel was most unhappy about recent developments, but pride made him unwilling to give an inch. He came immediately to Shargould, however, when word came that the new baby was about to be born. Two stubborn people were able to swallow their pride enough to rejoice together over the safe arrival of their beautiful new babe and the older children were overjoyed with their new sibling.

Hephzibah had been thankful that publicly Daniel continued to support her and nothing was ever openly discussed with fellow planters about the highly unusual arrangements on the Townsend plantation. Many of their relatives and neighbors certainly had their own opinions, but at least managed to keep their tongues between their teeth and not verbalize them. A number of the women on neighboring plantations secretly admired Hephzibah's courageous stance in the midst of a man's world where women were expected to know their place and graciously stay in it. Each woman realized that she personally would not dare do as Hephzibah had done, but nonetheless silently applauded her stand. When any dared hint at the subject, wanting so much to inquire what had led to such a pass, one speaking look from Mrs. Townsend's fine eyes stopped the words before they were formed.

Meanwhile, the children learned to cope with their unusual situation. Each evening the family dined together at Bleak Hall, and each evening came the trek back to Shargould for Hephzibah and the children.

Tragedy never seemed far away for the Townsend family and Christmas 1820 was one ever after remembered as scarred by sorrow. Precious little sprite Sarah Calder had only celebrated her fourth birthday in October, but on Christmas Eve she was hit with a sudden and virulent attack of dysentery, and all the doctor's tender ministrations were to no effect. None would forget the Christmas of 1820, for early in the morning following that day that was usually so full of joy, Sarah was no more. Before the new year arrived, Hephzibah and Daniel stood weeping yet again at the side of another child's grave.

Mary and Susan were thankful for each other's company when they settled in at Madame Demings Boarding School in Charleston. Susan and Maria Furman were day students there, and lifelong friendships were formed among the four girls. The younger Townsend children were still studying with a tutor and were continuing the habit that appeared to be the norm for the Townsend children: The girls attended church with their mother, and the boys with their father. Daniel was highly gratified in 1821 when a new minister came to their Presbyterian congregation, the Reverend William States Lee, who proved to be a favorite among islanders and put down lasting roots in the community. Reverend Lee and Hephzibah developed an enduring friendship as well, and he proved supportive of Baptist endeavors on Edisto, whereas Hephzibah always lent moral support to the Presbyterian membership.

The great majority of those attending Edisto Baptist Church were slaves, along with several plantation mistresses who were part of the mite society and a sprinkling of men. Some of the planters were affronted by the fact that all who attended the little church were free to sit where they wished and looked askance at such a custom. Such practices did not fit their sense of what was proper in this highly polarized society. There was none, however, who voiced such sentiments around Sister Townsend. She could say more without words than anyone they knew could convey by talking full spate.

Hephzibah personally found it difficult to understand her own beloved Charleston pastor's stance on slaves. She had read a paper Dr. Furman had written early in his ministry calling slavery "an undoubted evil," and yet he now seemed paternalistic in his views of slaves and owned several himself. On the other hand, Furman always exhibited a deep concern for their souls and made a practice of instructing young slave children in the Scriptures. This certainly happened nowhere else on Edisto.

Just recently however, Furman wrote a paper addressed to the state's governor, explaining the "views" of Baptists relative to the colored population. Whereas early in his life Furman talked of slavery's inherent evil and hoped that in time it would naturally disappear, Hephzibah could not help but feel his voice of conscience was now stilled by the economic expediencies of this area in which he lived.

On the other hand, Hephzibah was honest with herself and understood that in spite of her own strong regard for what was just, she herself did not take a stand in accordance with what her heart told her was the Christlike stance where slavery was concerned. Her largest comfort was that their little church, and certainly Baptists as a whole, were honestly concerned with the soul condition of every person in involuntary servitude. That was a start.

But then in May 1822, Charleston — and indeed the whole low country — was shocked by the thwarted slave revolt in that city. Denmark Vesey, a free black citizen for some twenty years, was said to have planned and organized a major rebellion, intending to kill plantation owners and escape to freedom in Haiti. Of all things, he was a leader in a black Presbyterian church and used the church as a planning location. One of the slaves involved in the plot informed on Vesey, and the revolt was stopped before it started. By July, Denmark Vesey was hanged, and a spirit of mistrust and fear walked the streets of Charleston.

Daniel was quick to remind his wife of the dangers of "freeing people who didn't know their place." She was in no mood to discuss a subject that was always a sensitive topic between the two of them, something each realized they could never agree upon. Townsend hinted that the kind of freedom Hephzibah "was allowing" in her Baptist church was just looking for trouble, just as was her notion of educating the Townsend slaves. One long smoldering look from those deep dark eyes, accompanied by not one word, stopped the conversation right there.

A number of eyebrows were raised in 1822 when forty-two-year-old Hephzibah Jenkins gave birth to her fifteenth child. Daniel Townsend was now a sixty-three-year-old patriarch, and although the two clearly lived in separate houses, they were just as clearly still very much a couple. The healthy little boy was named for a much-admired friend of the family, Richard Furman, who happily stood as godfather to his tiny namesake.

The Townsends maintained their relationship and two residences, but sometimes Hephzibah despaired of Daniel ever coming to terms with what she considered the only just thing to do: Honor each of their children with a legacy. She saw no other answer that she could find acceptable. By law, she could not take back what the law declared was her dowry to be administered by the husband. She could only stand firm and pray for divine intervention.

Occasionally, however, Hephzibah felt a ray of hope in those moments when Daniel would perform some task of considerable kindness to help her in a situation in which she knew he personally did not have an interest. Such was the case when he listened to her entreaty to give fourteen acres of land near Shargould to the Baptist church in Charleston as a gift in perpetuity to support a pastor for her beloved church. With him to sign along with her, the papers were completely legal and binding, and it gave her deep satisfaction to know he was willing to make the gesture. Maybe there was still some hope of him eventually changing his will.

The joy that both Hephzibah and Daniel felt in this last beautiful child, however, was to remain a shockingly short time. In 1823, both the baby and Hephzibah contracted malaria and were deathly ill. Hephzibah had strong recuperative powers, and was able to fight off the fever's deadly effects. No so little Richard; within a matter of days he was gone, and the sorrow in Hephzibah's heart returned in full force. How could she bear the loss of so many these years, each one infinitely precious? Weakened by the debilitating effects of malaria, she would spend hours weeping in helpless anguish. Yet once more, though painfully slowly, that indomitable spirit came to the fore, and Hephzibah accepted what must be accepted and stood shaking with silent grief in the family graveyard that now held far too many beloved children. Only the thought of reunion in heaven with each beloved one could ease her aching heart.

～ Twenty-Four ～

1823-1829
THE TOWNSEND CLAN

Mary Frampton and Susan Martha returned to Edisto from finishing school in 1823, polished and poised young women, much courted and admired by the young men of the island as well as several in Charleston and on adjoining islands. They also continued their rich friendship with Susan and Maria Furman, realizing how very much they had in common. The following year, Mary and Susan Townsend both were baptized by Richard Furman, and it was a moment of special joy for their mother. Hephzibah frequently spent weekends now in Charleston, and the girls usually accompanied her. Later in the year Mary Frampton began to be seriously courted by handsome young John Theus Pope of St. Helena Island. Mary, with her speaking dark eyes and shining black hair, was a true belle, but she appeared truly smitten this time. She was especially gratified that John was also a Baptist.

Susan Martha was a popular young woman as well. She seemed taken with her favorite young beau — so taken, in fact, that they soon became engaged. Then, just when Hephzibah was thinking that there might be two weddings at the same time in the family, the situation changed. Susan's young man was a strong Presbyterian, and Susan Martha Townsend, very much her

Her Way

mother's daughter, was every bit as staunch a Baptist. Their discussions grew quite heated and came to a crux when Susan realized he had no intention of changing his denomination. Nor did she. Her faith and beliefs were a fundamental part of her makeup and she was not willing to compromise. Susan bid her fiancé a sad goodbye, and, to her worried mother's mind, she seemed to "hang up her courting dresses" in the closet and did not once again evince interest in any young man.

Susan did, however, serve as maid of honor in Mary Frampton's wedding to John Pope in January of 1824. Hephzibah and Bella were at their best, preparing a beautiful wedding cake and all the trimmings for a magnificent island wedding. Then the radiant bride and groom were off on their wedding trip before beginning their lives together on St. Helena. The Popes set up housekeeping on John's property, Feliciana, a comfortable plantation dwelling on the nearby island. And on October 30, forty-four-year-old Hephzibah Townsend became a grandmother for the first time when Mary Townsend Pope gave birth to her little girl, appropriately named Hephzibah Jenkins Pope. That grandmother's heart swelled with pride when she took her own young brood for their first visit to see their new niece.

Susan Martha no longer expressed interest in any of the young men who seemed attracted to her, but she began a new endeavor that was to give her great satisfaction and a sense of usefulness for which she had been longing. Susan organized the first Sunday school on Edisto Island in 1824. In fact, the idea of a Sunday school was quite a new one anywhere, and Susan recognized a need for training the children when they were quite young.

Each weekend, Susan would gather together children in the little white frame building that housed Edisto Baptist Church, and there would be a sea of eager young faces looking up at her. Several of them were children of island planters, including Susan's younger siblings, and dozens of eager young black faces. They all were excited to be learning real Bible stories and how heroes of long ago were really just like people in the low country now. Miss Susan got the children involved and encouraged competition to see who could memorize the most Scripture. The teacher's favorite times were when the little ones stood to recite, and hearing their young voices quoting Bible passages was a particular joy to her.

John Ferrars stayed busy managing the family plantations on Wadmalaw and at the same time expending a lot of energy on South Carolina politics. He was quite passionate about the issue of states' rights. Daniel was proud of his son's political acumen, but his mother's heart was much disquieted by John's strident attitude. Amarinthia was a beautiful young teenager now and, like all the girls, felt a special bond with her mother. She was already enjoying being part of the mite society and was a budding writer, faithfully recording impressions and ideas in her journal. Amarinthia tended to be quiet and reserved, but was beginning to attract interest among the young beaus on Edisto. Brilliant young Daniel Jenkins was studying hard as he prepared to go away to college. Daniel loved delving into science and was fascinated with how the human body worked. His observant mother felt she was watching a doctor in the making.

The younger children had a healthy competition going in the classroom. Benjamin was a quiet young teenager, enjoying spending as much time possible outdoors, riding and hunting. The youngest of all the brood, young Theodora Elizabeth, was "Lizzie" to nearly everyone except her mama, who always called her "Elizabeth." Realizing this was the last child she would have, Hephzibah felt unusually close to her. Hephzibah often noted the special bond existing between Susan and little Elizabeth. She smiled as she recalled so clearly the closeness of her own bond with 'Rinthia, where there had been such an age difference that she felt much like her sister's mother. Just so did Susan respond to Elizabeth and mother her.

Another child to have a special share of Hephzibah Townsend's love and attention was Bella's son Lewis. To Bella's sorrow, she was unable to have more children, but Lewis was her pride and joy. Not only did he excel in the plantation classroom but also quickly learned carpentering from his skilled father. Then tragedy hit the little cabin standing so close to Bleak Hall. Joseph was injured in a freak accident while cutting lumber, and all the doctor's considerable skills were not enough to save his life. A grieving Bella quietly went about her work around Bleak Hall and the tabby ovens, but a stricken look remained in her eyes for many months to come. In turn, Hephzibah grieved for Bella's sorrow, but was at a loss as to how to comfort her. At the same time, she determined that every advantage that could be given young Lewis would be afforded him. For a young teenager, his skills were quite unusual, and Lewis was already carving a place for himself in the plantation carpentry shop. Hephzibah was now doubly grateful that Bella had such a stalwart son to comfort and help her.

Hephzibah and Daniel, along with most of the planters on

Edisto, were excited when they learned that the eminent Marquis de Lafayette was to actually visit their little island. William Seabrook had asked for the honor of hosting the Marquis and invited all the leading planters to come for a special dinner. Hephzibah relished every moment of the special occasion, thinking throughout the entire evening of how Papa would love to have been here for this moment, celebrating one of the real heroes of the Revolution. The highlight of the day came when Seabrook asked Lafayette to do the honors in naming their newborn. His wife, Emma, placed her child in the arms of the Marquis, who smiled into the little face and promptly named her Carolina Lafayette. The entire evening was one of the bright spots in the fabric of their lives, never to be forgotten.

However, some new kind of sorrow often seemed to arise without warning. So was the case that August. Susan Furman wrote to Susan Martha about her father's serious illness. Susan Martha quickly scanned the letter, then silently handed it to her mother; Hephzibah was stricken with fear that her beloved pastor was desperately ill. Susan Furman's letter explained that her father had been moving much more slowly lately and was suffering severe stomach pain. The previous summer, much sickness and death had hit Charleston, and Furman's medical skills and ability to provide spiritual comfort kept him busy long hours each day. In the months to follow, he had not seemed able to recover his own strength. Now this August of 1825, as he daily grew weaker, he received the sad news that his dear friend these many years, Charles Cotesworth Pinckney, had just died. That was like an additional blow to Furman.

Susan Martha shared the alarming news with all the family at the evening meal, and Townsend himself grew concerned, for over the years he and Richard Furman had forged a true friendship based on deep mutual respect. The family prayed and waited for more word, and it arrived all too soon. Susan Furman wrote another letter: Her cherished father died the morning of August 25. She wrote, however, not just of his suffering but also of his bright faith. Susan was able to be at his bedside. Furman asked for her to read Psalm 23, and while hearing it he slipped into eternity. Upon reading the letter, Hephzibah felt as if she had received another blow; her beloved pastor was no more, her friend, her support, her bastion of encouragement. This was yet another piece of the fabric of her life now gone.

The family made plans to go to Charleston for the memorial service. Prior to the time for the service, Hephzibah was grateful to have an hour to spend with Rachel, who had arrived from Sumter to be with the rest of Furman's children. Being the oldest daughter, Rachel could share with Hephzibah special memories of her father's early years.

It was a difficult month on several fronts. While in Charleston, Hephzibah also spent several hours with her childhood friend, Eliza Izard. Dear Eliza had already lost her husband with a sudden illness just three years earlier, and now her father, Charles Pinckney, was no more. It was a somber boat ride home for the Townsends following the Charleston visit, with Hephzibah quietly mourning the loss of her spiritual mentor and stalwart partner in ministry. That remarkable man had made possible the rebirth of a Baptist church on Edisto, and she felt bereft of his wise leadership.

Also on the missionary society front, all of the women were on tenterhooks, wondering what news might come next from the Judsons in Burmah. Any news was painfully slow in arriving, always months behind the actual happenings. Each time Hephzibah received a new issue of *Missionary Magazine,* she seized upon it and quickly scanned for news about the Judsons and their harrowing circumstances. Finally in mid-1826, the new magazine reached Edisto that word had just come from Calcutta: The Judsons were still living. What their condition might be, no one knew.

At each meeting of the society, the anxious question always came: What about the Judsons? By the end of the year, the most recent edition of the magazine finally reached Edisto: The Judsons were indeed alive. Adoniram was imprisoned in two different death prisons for nearly two years, but Ann somehow managed to keep him alive. When Hephzibah read the news aloud, the women broke into applause upon learning that their missionaries had survived. The meeting turned into a celebration.

It was to be short-lived joy. The next issue of the magazine bore the news that Ann Hasseltine Judson was too weak to fight off the attack of spinal meningitis that devastated her already weakened body. She died in October 1826, and Adoniram was left to grieve alone. The women seated around the parlor hearing this shocking news felt like they had lost a family member, so closely did their hearts embrace these, their first missionaries.

Hephzibah was able to give thanks that same year, nonetheless, for a new source of spiritual encouragement, because in 1826, First Baptist Church called Basil Manly as its pastor. In fact, just before Richard Furman's death, he recommended young Reverend Manly to succeed him, and, to Hephzibah, that alone put the seal of approval on Charleston's new minister.

There was a special winsomeness about Manly's personality and a profound spiritual depth. These, combined with his genuine warmth and concern for others, made him a worthy successor. In no time, Hephzibah realized that she had a new friend in this young man of God, one with a listening ear and loving heart. Then the special tie with the Townsends was further strengthened when Pastor Manly baptized Amarinthia shortly before her sixteenth birthday. He visited the Edisto church when he had opportunity, but Manly's time was painfully limited. He did agree with Sister Townsend, as he always called her, that indeed, Edisto Church needed a pastor there on the island to minister to the flock, and he set about to help make that happen.

The maintenance of two separate households continued to stretch on for the Townsends. When Hephzibah first made the move to Shargould, she kept hoping that the issue of Daniel's will could be satisfactorily settled quite quickly. That didn't happen. Sometimes she despaired of Daniel ever swallowing his pride long enough to be willing to rewrite that will and share their holdings with all the children. To Daniel, it appeared to be a matter of pride; to Hephzibah, it was very much one of fairness. She saw no way that all their land going to their oldest son could be fair to their other children. Nonetheless, the two Townsend households had ceased to be a topic of conversation around the island, and was now looked upon as a matter of course.

Then about this time, her husband performed an act of

great kindness that rekindled hope in Hephzibah's heart that he would eventually come around about the will. It seemed like that particular chasm of disagreement had been there forever. One day, and with no prior discussion, Daniel did an unprecedented thing: Knowing how disturbed Hephzibah had been these twenty or more years over the disputed church property, he managed to purchase that property outright from fellow planter William Seabrook. This generous act brought a great sense of relief to Hephzibah's mind, and gave her hope that Daniel might eventually see eye to eye with her about the will.

Second son Daniel Jenkins was a promising seven-teen-year-old now and excited about going away to school at Harvard. Massachusetts sounded a world away, and Daniel looked upon this as an adventure. Hephzibah had a special rapport with this second son to survive, and his going so far away was very difficult for her.

Then word came in 1829 that it looked like there would be a pastor for Edisto Baptist Church. When Hephzibah first heard the news, she was truly excited; she had waited so long for this to happen. A Rev. Peter Ludlow of Connecticut had moved south because of his poor health, and for a short time was pastor of the church in Georgetown. Then it appeared he would accept the pulpit at Edisto Church. Pastor Ludlow preached his first message in November and as soon as he began speaking, Hephzibah looked around and noticed the startled expressions on the faces of the scores of slaves seated in the congregation. Reverend Ludlow's accent was one never before heard by these people in the low country, most of whom had roots in West Africa and spoke the rich Gullah dialect. "Northern" English was close to a foreign language to their ears. Hephzibah simply trusted that in due time they would grow familiar with his clipped type of speech, so unlike the warm and liquid tones with which they were familiar.

Not only his speech but his manner was also quite different. There was a type of southern pleasantness of manner and informality that most Edisto Islanders simply took for granted among themselves. Their way of life was quite laid back and, just so, their speech. On the other hand, there was about Pastor Ludlow an aura of formality, a stiffness of manner that Hephzibah Townsend hoped would moderate over time. Nor did he seem to be in good health, even though only in his early thirties. Furthermore, Reverend Ludlow's manner toward Hephzibah herself — in fact, toward all women — seemed quite formal and forbidding, even bordering on condescending. Again, she trusted this would change over time as the pastor grew more familiar with them. The best thing would be for the new pastor and his wife to actually move to Edisto and settle down to work among the people here. However, as the months went by, it appeared this was not going to happen. Time would tell, but Hephzibah could not help a tiny frisson of doubt as she considered this inauspicious beginning for their first official pastor at Edisto Baptist.

— *Twenty-Five* —

1829-1834

MOVING HOME

It was not in Hephzibah Townsend's nature to be a carrier of tales. She abhorred gossip and normally chose to bite her tongue and ignore whatever couldn't be changed with kind words or positive actions. Nevertheless, the growing problems with Pastor Ludlow were an ever-present concern. She did not want to burden an overly busy Pastor Manly with problems on Edisto. Furthermore, the busy mistress of Bleak Hall and leader of the Mite Society had far too much on her plate to idly spend time in stirring coals of dissent. Business was nearly more than she and Bella could handle, even with all those who helped them, but the funds provided well for church needs and offerings to the society, which had now expanded to provide money for ministerial education.

However, by 1832 the situation with Pastor Ludlow was increasingly disquieting. He was irregular in his visits to Edisto and he made no pretense about his condescending attitude toward what he clearly considered the weaker sex. Ludlow bitterly resented what he called the influence of Hephzibah Townsend in the church and felt she went far beyond what he considered "a woman's place." Nor did he feel the need to spend much time on the concerns of the slave membership who made up the great preponderance of the church. This was a gnawing worry to Hephzibah, who cringed at Pastor Ludlow's callous attitude, but she could not bring herself to criticize him to her Charleston pastor.

Dr. Manly visited Edisto Baptist as frequently as he could, and it was he, as pastor of the mother church, who baptized new believers. Hephzibah and 'Rinthia were beaming on April 9 when Dr. Manly and a Brother Reynolds from Charleston heard the experiences of the forty-three who had trusted the Lord. Many planters came for the occasion of the baptisms and to hear Dr. Manly preach; most of them had slaves numbered among those being baptized that day.

The Townsend clan continued to expand as more grand-children were born. Mary was not only mother to a growing brood of young Popes but was also leading out in the establishment of the Baptist church in Beaufort District. Hephzibah found it inter-esting that Baptists seemed to thrive on St. Helena, whereas on Edisto the great majority of planters considered Baptists as far too unconscious of class distinction to be seriously considered as a denomination.

Mary's younger sisters Susan and Amarinthia had not yet married, and both were very active at the church with their mother. To the continued surprise of most of her family, Susan made no bones about being uninterested in matrimony. Surely it was the goal of a young woman to marry and have a home of her own. Hephzibah had a feeling, although she did not express it openly, that Susan Martha simply preferred her independence. If that was her choice, her mother supported her wholeheartedly.

Son Daniel was thriving in his classes at Harvard and was

studying medicine, determined to be a doctor upon graduation. Hephzibah was looking forward to the time he would come back to the low country. John Ferrars was enjoying his role as a planter and had still made no efforts toward matrimony. But then, Hephzibah reflected, nor had his father been in a rush. Daniel had been thirty-seven when they married. John was engrossed in politics, particularly the issue of Nullification. He was ardently concerned about states' rights, feeling that a state has the right to nullify any federal law that the state deemed unconstitutional.

His mother realized that the issue of slavery was much on this son's mind, for voices from the North were becoming increasingly strident about the need for abolition in the United States. John Ferrars wrote a long and passionate letter to former President James Madison, the brilliant leader most responsible for the framing of the Constitution. John felt he would find sympathetic ears in President Madison and was asking him to speak out for Nullification.

By the time news reached Edisto about the Nat Turner Rebellion in Virginia, planters in all states grew increasingly uneasy. A number of plantation owners and their families were killed in Virginia, and although the rebellion was quickly put down, there was a sense of foreboding traveling in its wake. Daniel was so upset over that issue that he dared to bring up the subject of the rebellion with Hephzibah, and yet again she tried to make him understand how she felt. When Townsend expressed his worries over "all those freedoms you allow our slaves," Hephzibah confronted him, "Daniel, have you ever had a slave at Bleak Hall disrespect you, or lash out in anger, or get out of what you call his place?" Her voice was heated with emotion.

Daniel paused, cleared his throat and admitted, "Not really."

Hephzibah was passionate in her wish to get her husband to truly understand her perspective. Tears welled up in her eyes as she pled with him, "Daniel, can't you understand my heart? Maum Jean and Jack literally saved my life." She fought to maintain her composure, "I mean it when I say these are my people. Please just try to show a compassionate heart." Tears trickled down her cheeks, and Daniel was not proof against the obvious pain reflected on her face.

Daniel begged, "Don't weep, Hephzibah, please don't weep. I do try to understand you; it is simply hard for me to grasp." He heaved a sigh, "I just didn't grow up feeling that way like you did." So in spite of their lack of agreement, each felt the other at least listened.

Even when the two disagreed on a principle, just such moments of accord renewed Hephzibah's long-held hope that Daniel might yet change his will to include all of his children. It seemed like this contention over the will had been around forever. It had certainly been there a dozen years already. It was like a knife cutting through their relationship, always just beneath the surface of their daily lives, never far from either of their minds.

By late 1832, Hephzibah was growing increasingly worried about the antipathy she sensed in Pastor Ludlow. She was beginning to dread those Sundays when he came to preach, and this tore at her heart because she loved her church. 'Rinthia was extremely sensitive to the atmosphere as well, and there seemed a sense of uneasiness among many of the members who were slaves. Then Hephzibah heard rumblings from chance remarks let drop by Reverend Ludlow about dissatisfaction among leaders in the association with the state of affairs at Edisto Baptist Church, all those slave members and only two white women with no leadership from island planters. It appeared those men resented her position and the fact that she had failed to increase the male leadership.

And then in December 1832, Hephzibah received a vitriolic four-page letter from Peter Ludlow. It became obvious that he had avoided any discussion of this matter with Dr. Manly, but instead had enlisted support from two men in the association who resented any hint of leadership by a mere woman who should know her "place" better than that. When Hephzibah Townsend opened that letter she was stunned. They were undertaking to dissolve Edisto Baptist Church. How could it be? She read on:

> *Madam, As the result of much prayerful delib-*
> *eration, the church has instructed me to address*
> *you once more in your connexion with them.*
> *They have for a long time felt exceedingly embar-*
> *rassed in their minds with respect to the path of*
> *duty ... the church has instructed me to demand*
> *of you. I now do demand-1st the immediate*
> *surrender of all the property of every sort which*
> *you have in your keeping belonging of right to*
> *them ... and 2ndly, that you henceforth keep*
> *within your own proper place in the church,*
> *demeaning yourself with the modesty, humility*

and propriety which as a female member of the
New Testament requires of you.

Ludlow continued in the same disparaging tone for four long pages, signing himself: "With becoming respect, I am, Madam, Yr. humble pastor and friend, P Ludlow, Pastor Edisto Island Baptist Church."

Hephzibah sat in shock for the longest time. This was nearly too much to absorb. Gathering her wits about her, she fell to her knees in prayer and sought divine leadership. Next, she attempted to possess her soul in patience and decide just what to do. Hephzibah realized that she was different in her personal sense of justice and her outspokenness as a woman. Well, she knew the prevailing male attitude. But, again, she knew of the staunch support and loyalty her own husband gave her. Daniel once more came to the rescue, and one of his first actions was to write their lawyer, Thomas Grimke, for legal advice. John Ferrars, in his position as a state senator, also did the same. Father and son might frequently deplore their loved one's headstrong character, but invariably they surrounded her with support.

Wanting to get to the bottom of things, Hephzibah met with Pastor Manly at the first opportunity. Manly knew nothing of the actions Ludlow had taken, and the elders — a Mr. Holmes and Mr. Husser — were part of Charleston Baptist Association but certainly not speaking on behalf of First Baptist Church. Manly realized this grew out of Reverend Ludlow's personal distrust of Hephzibah and his deep resentment of her standing in Edisto Church, taking away from what he considered should be the leadership role that was rightly his as pastor. Manly also realized a fact that probably had not occurred to Hephzibah Townsend. There was about her a certain *presence*. This was a woman of indomitable spirit, a person of unquestioned strength. Basil Manly strongly suspected that Peter Ludlow felt intimidated around her.

For her part, Hephzibah also contacted Lawyer Grimke. Shortly thereafter, Hephzibah felt a great sense of relief when she learned that the Charleston association refused to dissolve Edisto Baptist Church. The situation dragged on longer, but in order to prevent any further such problem, Hephzibah and 'Rinthia were able to convey the interests of Edisto Baptist through three male trustees — including 'Rinthia's husband, William, who obligingly moved his membership from the Charleston church to Edisto. This rather spiked the guns of Ludlow and those who had backed his efforts to dissolve the church in which Hephzibah had invested more than twenty years of her life.

It later was made official by the Charleston association that Edisto Baptist was recognized as a church in full standing, and Hephzibah rejoiced over answered prayer. The designs of Providence continued to be manifest when Peter Ludlow, in steadily failing health, decided to return to Connecticut and his family there. Sister Townsend felt like a great load had been lifted off her heart and she once more took courage.

Basil Manly himself realized that all the happenings with Ludlow and the church were a testimony to Hephzibah Townsend's exceptional position. Many characteristics might be deplored in a woman — traits like assertiveness, exercising leadership, or making unilateral decisions. However, there was a virtue that was universally admired in a proper Christian lady, and that was obedience to the will of God. There was no one in Baptist circles who doubted the overpowering strength of this woman's conviction and determination.

Manly also understood the unique contribution made by the Edisto church to the enslaved population of the island. Edisto planters were not willing for their slaves to officially be members of the Charleston church, but were happy to allow them to belong to the nearby Edisto flock. The custom was that owners would give their servants permission slips allowing them to be baptized into the membership of Edisto Baptist Church. By this time, the church had well over one hundred slave members, far more than belonged to any other church on the island.

As Hephzibah looked back on the deep waters through which she had come, she gave thanks repeatedly for the way God had preserved His church. She also deeply appreciated the help of both her husband and her oldest son, who, although not part of her work at Edisto Baptist, were willing nonetheless to come to her aid and step in to provide the necessary male voice during this period of time where women *had* no voice. Daniel settled the entire matter when he and Hephzibah jointly gave in perpetuity to the church the deed for the property where the church stood. In the years to come, this preserved the church for those members who had no legal voice of their own.

Even in the middle of all the angst about preserving their beloved church, 1833 turned out to be a banner year in Hephzibah's book of memories for a reason very close to her heart. Matters over Daniel's will came to a crux. In March, just about the time a touch of spring began asserting itself in flowers springing up and warm rays of sunshine touching every surface with new life, Hephzibah seemed to sense a new touch of lightness in Daniel's manner. She hoped and prayed that was a good sign.

Many a long hour in the stillness of the nights was spent in prayer for God to work a miracle and allow them to reach the right decision. Hephzibah was very aware that it was long out of her hands, and she could only cling to hope that change would come before it was too late. Daniel was seventy-four now and was slowing down. She was grateful that John Ferrars was taking increasing responsibility for keeping the various plantations functioning and profitable. Daniel had trained him well. But that didn't help their other children, with no provision for them in years to come.

In her moments of self-reflection, Hephzibah readily admitted to herself that she was more than tired of living at Shargould and running the household at Bleak Hall at the same time. She was much younger than Daniel, but felt every one of her own fifty-three years. Small wonder he was feeling his mortality. One March evening following dinner, Daniel beckoned his wife to go to the library with him. Taking a deep breath and masking her inner butterflies with an outward tranquility, Hephzibah did as he wished. Closing the door behind them, Daniel slowly walked to his desk, cluttered as it was by scattered letters and files, and opened the center drawer.

Pulling out a document, Daniel courteously asked Hephzibah to be seated and silently handed her the papers. Hephzibah began to read: "The Will of Daniel Townsend of Edisto Island in Parish of St. Johns Colleton." As Hephzibah's eyes quickly scanned down the sheet of paper, her eyes clouded with tears and she could scarcely read through the blur. Daniel had bequeathed property to each of their children, and divided all their holdings up in a fair and just way, also taking care to provide most generously for her own wishes. Silently, she reached out to embrace her husband, and they clung to each other in a rush of relief and thankfulness.

"Daniel," she began when once more she could form words, "what can I say except I thank you. I thank you," and she choked on her emotions. Very little more composed than she, Daniel gruffly responded, "Hephzibah, I'm a stubborn old man, but God knows I want to be a fair one. You have been my stalwart companion for all these years" — and here he paused with a small quirk of his lips — "and, yes, I proposed to a beautiful young woman about thirty-eight years ago because I had fallen in love with all of who she was, and that included," and here he smiled outright, "her force of character and her sense of justice all rolled into one small and remarkable person."

When Hephzibah could collect her scattered thoughts, she framed his weathered face in her small hands as she smiled into his eyes, "And, Mr. Townsend, I can't wait to move back to Bleak Hall, and know that home is home once more!"

Letter from Hephzibah Townsend to Thomas Grimke, 1833. (Courtesy James B. Duke Library, Furman University, Greenville, South Carolina.)

— Twenty-Six —

1834-1839

A FAMILY GROWN

Where on earth have the years gone? Hephzibah mused as she watched Elizabeth excitedly packing her trunks for Charleston and finishing school. This youngest Townsend daughter was especially proud of the dainty little trunk Lewis had crafted for her, with her initials TET in shiny brass studs on the top. She was feeling very grownup at fourteen. Elizabeth tucked away in one of her trunks the beautiful tree of life quilt that she and Mama made last year, with its colorful birds and intricate stitching. All the girls knew the art of quilting, for Hephzibah passed on what she learned from Aunt Abby.

Elizabeth would be boarding with Pastor Manly and his family, and that in itself was exciting, for she loved and admired this special family friend who recently baptized her. Conversely, Hephzibah was secretly dreading Elizabeth's departure for the city. This was her baby, no matter Elizabeth was already a glowing young woman.

All of the family seemed to heave a metaphorical sigh of relief after the trouble over the will was settled. The children lost some of the tautness of family relationships their parents' separation caused all those years, for Hephzibah was once more home permanently at Bleak Hall and all was well. John Ferrars and Mary were grown and gone, and Daniel Jenkins close to receiving his medical degree. Susan and Amarinthia were busy helping their mother with church functions and were actively assisting with the mite society. Ben was a bit of a maverick, preferring not to go to college, but busy helping his father around the plantation and spending as much time as he could outside riding and hunting. This youngest son seemed most at home on the back of a horse.

And now here was the family's baby, headed off to finishing school. Life seemed to be rushing by too quickly for Hephzibah, who never had to worry about idle time, what with her responsibilities running Bleak Hall in addition to church and mite society activities and operating a thriving business. A dozen times a day, she mentally gave thanks for Bella — not just a trusted servant, but much more a dear friend and business partner. At the same time, Bella was thankful to be busy and worked hard at not dwelling on her grief over Joseph, but rather giving thanks for Lewis and staying occupied with the baking that she loved and at which she excelled. Miz Hephzibah frequently reminded her that without her invaluable skills and gifts of organization, neither the church nor the society would be functioning properly. *In the eyes of the world,* Bella often inwardly mused, *I am a slave. But in my heart I am God's own child and important to His work.* Such thoughts were her daily comfort.

Although life around Bleak Hall quickly regained its steady tenor, tragedy seemed determined to dog the footsteps of Hephzibah and Daniel Townsend. Late one evening, one of the servants rushed to Bleak Hall with the news that Massa Ben's horse had returned to the stables without a rider. Ben was an expert horseman, so the news struck fear in the hearts of his anxious parents. Daniel joined a troupe of servants who immediately left to search for him. Within the hour, a white-faced Daniel Townsend returned with the shocking news: Ben must have taken a fall from the horse near the marshes. It appeared the horse stumbled and Ben was thrown from its back. His head hit a rock, and their son never regained consciousness.

Two days later, a weeping and shaken mother and father stood together at the Jenkins family cemetery and saw the body of their grown son laid in the earth next to a row of his siblings. The entire household was so overcome with grief that it was many weeks before anyone could have a semblance of normality about their daily routine. Hephzibah's anguished heart wondered yet again how much sorrow a body could come to bear. Surely her grief was too heavy.

But, of course, the sun came up each morning as usual, the birds began singing at dawn, and life had to be lived. Yet somehow, the pain never quite went away, and again Hephzibah cried out silently, *Oh God, just help me number my days that I can apply my heart to wisdom.* How many of those days might there be? No one knew.

Nonetheless, news about missions endeavors was encouraging. After nearly twenty-five years of praying and giving, the Wadmalaw-Edisto Mite Society felt like the Judsons were a real part of all they did. The ladies rejoiced when word reached them in 1835 that just months earlier Adoniram Judson, a widower for eight long years, married the widowed young missionary Sarah Boardman. The Judsons were fascinating to these women in the low country, who felt like they personally had an investment in faraway Burmah where the work was expanding and new converts were being added.

Then missionary news felt even closer to home for them when the society learned that lovely young Henrietta Hall of Virginia had married her sweetheart, Lewis Shuck, and two weeks later sailed for China. The Shucks were America's first missionaries to that ancient kingdom. The ladies looked at each other in amazement and exclaimed over the bravery of this young bride, only seventeen years old yet willing to leave the only home she had ever known to go plant her life in a mysterious land far away.

There were also weddings much nearer to home, and the next one in the Townsend family was their doctor son. Daniel Jenkins was a newly minted physician with his degree from the prestigious Harvard College, and he was settling down with Miss Henrietta Evans of St. Paul's Parish. Hephzibah regretted not being able to prepare the wedding reception since the ceremony took place at the bride's home, but she enjoyed the service this time without needing to feel responsible for any preparations.

Then news of an impending wedding on Edisto brought excitement to Bleak Hall. John Ferrars had reached the age of thirty-six as a bachelor. However, his father had married at thirty-seven, so the son had not waited quite as long. John's bride was a cousin, lovely and gentle Miss Caroline Jenkins. Of course, Hephzibah and Bella catered the wedding and it was an all-island event. The newlyweds would live on one of the family plantations on Wadmalaw, and John Ferrars would continue to manage several Townsend properties. He was already an expert in growing

Sea Island Cotton and recently invented a horse-drawn skimmer plow that was quite effective.

John was their oldest child and Elizabeth the youngest, and Hephzibah wondered how long before the baby of the family would start talking about marriage. Elizabeth was clearly excited on her latest trip home, talking about Thomas Peter Smith, the young man who was a frequent visitor in the Manly home. He was already an up-and-coming businessman and very active at First Baptist Church. Elizabeth's fond mother didn't attempt to dampen her daughter's enthusiasm, but did allow herself to frequently say, "Elizabeth, that is lovely and we would like to meet him sometime." And she usually added, "Remember now, you are still in school and there is plenty of time." Just as frequently, Hephzibah reminded herself that when she was sixteen, as Elizabeth now was, she was already married and expecting her first baby.

Wedding bells seemed to linger in the fragrant breezes that drifted through the flowers clustering around Bleak Hall, for in 1836, the twenty-eight-year-old Amarinthia finally fell in love. Like her mother, Amarinthia was a staunch Baptist, but in deference to her father, she and Isaac Jenkins Mikell were married in Edisto Presbyterian Church, with a beaming Rev. William States Lee performing the ceremony, and Hephzibah and Bella again outdoing themselves with a beautiful reception at Bleak Hall. Mikell owned several properties and was planning to build at Peter's Point. Hephzibah was especially delighted, for that was not very distant from the Townsends' own plantation. Susan and Elizabeth were both bridesmaids at the morning wedding. The two sisters were a contrast — Susan sounding pleased that she herself was not getting married, but young Elizabeth with visions of orange blossoms dancing in her daydreams.

Sad news came that autumn to the mite society, for late in September Hephzibah learned from Pastor Manly that the venerated Luther Rice, while on one of his trips to South Carolina, grew extremely ill after reaching Edgefield District. Manly had just learned that Rice, that noble leader in missions formation, died on September 25. Rice's body was lovingly placed to rest at the Pine Pleasant Baptist Church out of Edgefield and as the news spread, so did Baptists far and wide mourn the unexpected death of their beloved leader. Luther Rice was only fifty-three years old.

Hephzibah Townsend had long ago learned that nothing in life will long remain the same. In fact, she discovered through the years that the only known constant was her Heavenly Father, always in her heart, her Polar Star. Everything else seemed to fluctuate, and truth be known, she never found change all that easy. Sure enough, 1837 brought more change when Basil Manly resigned as pastor of First Baptist, Church — meaning, of course, he was lost to their Edisto church and its people as well. Dr. Manly was having increasing difficulty with his voice, and preaching so frequently became a real problem. Then just months ago, insistent pleading came from the University of Alabama to become their president.

Knowing this position would be less strain on his voice, Manly reluctantly made the decision to leave Charleston, his beloved church, and his many friends there. And once more, Hephzibah began to speculate on what God might have in store for their little Edisto flock. It was continuing to grow, with a scattering of white planters and ladies in attendance and many slaves, for whom the Baptist church was their hearts' home.

Young Elizabeth was able to make temporary arrangements for another place to live until she finished school, but she was already in love with her Thomas Peter Smith and eager for the day to come when they would marry. For her part, Hephzibah spent many a late night hour pondering the future of her church and the many slaves who made up most of the membership. Ever since Hephzibah had reached the age of reason, she had been trying to reconcile slavery with Christian principles. Just about the time she had convinced herself that she could live with things as they were, something would occur that would bring that gnawing sense of shame and unease back to her heart. Sometimes it helped to realize that her spiritual guides, both Dr. Furman and Dr. Manly, came to terms with the institution of slavery. Both were compassionate men who were deeply concerned about the souls of people, regardless of the color of their skin — but Hephzibah was an avid reader, and knew from an article Furman wrote back around the turn of the century that he regarded slavery as "undoubtedly an evil." Just so did Dr. Manly. When he was still a college student, Manly wrote a most logical renunciation of slavery and called for emancipation. And then somehow cultural pressures and economic expediencies came to bear, and the voice of conscience in these eminent men was quieted.

About this time, Hephzibah, who dearly loved to read and especially enjoyed history, came across an article about the letters of Abigail Adams, for whom she had a great admiration. In one of her letters to husband John, written just prior to the Revolution,

Abigail expressed herself succinctly by saying, "I wish most sincerely there was not a slave in the province." Abigail's words carried weight with Hephzibah and caused her conscience to suffer pangs yet again.

As if to heap coals of fire on her own head, a pamphlet fell into her hands on one of her Charleston trips in 1837. A soberly dressed young woman on the street near Hephzibah's town house passed her on the street one morning and quietly handed her a pamphlet. Hephzibah was just walking up to her door, and thrust the paper into her reticule. Later that evening, she happened across the paper and gave it a cursory glance. And then her eyes widened as she began to read. The pamphlet was written by Angelina Grimke. Why, Angelina was her own lawyer's younger sister! She had never met Angelina and her sister Sarah, but indeed she had heard of them. Everyone in Charleston had. The Grimkes were a wealthy and prominent slaveholding family. Their late father, John, had been the chief justice of South Carolina's Supreme Court and their brother Thomas a prominent lawyer.

As Hephzibah turned the pamphlet over in her hand, she recalled what she knew about the two sisters. Sarah was a bit younger than she, about 'Rinthia's age, and Angelina much younger, the age of Hephzibah's own Susan Martha. Hephzibah recalled hearing rumors that the Grimke sisters were not welcome in Charleston these days, that both had become Quakers, and that they were now abolitionists. She looked closely at the pamphlet, titled "An Appeal to the Christian Women of the South." Hephzibah was struck to the heart as she began reading Angelina's words of denunciation of the institution of slavery, telling how she grew up in a home with slaves and how her heart quailed within her when she saw a fellow human being whipped until the blood ran.

Hephzibah's mind immediately flew back to that long-ago summer day when she saw an overseer whipping an elderly slave. The pamphlet read, "Slavery is a canker sore, incessantly grieving." And Hephzibah Townsend's eyes filled with tears as she admitted the validity of that statement — and the picture never far from her conscious mind returned, the picture of her beloved Maum Jean as she lay dying, saying, "You, Miz Hephzibah, you body might be free, but you mind, unh unh." Hephzibah's heart burned with the crushing truth of those words, for in a very real sense she herself was enslaved by the system of slavery. The burden felt heavy.

Hephzibah had trouble sleeping that night, for the conflict in her heart raged on — torn between her life as it was, mistress of a large plantation and the owner of slaves and feeling bound by tradition and expediency, while on the other hand she knew it could not be right. Her conscience nearly overwhelmed her. Hephzibah could only agonize in prayer and ask God to help her do the best she could with the situation as she found it. "Oh God," she cried out in distress, "help me make a difference and do some good. I plead for strength and wisdom." At long last, she fell asleep, tears lingering on her cheeks.

Portrait of Maum Bella, now located at College of Charleston archives, Charleston, South Carolina. (Courtesy Addlestone Library, College of Charleston, Charleston, South Carolina.)

~ *Twenty-Seven* ~

1838-1842

DANIEL

Hephzibah Townsend loved weddings, and her favorite ones were those in her own family. It was Elizabeth's turn now, and Hephzibah was feeling nostalgic. This was her youngest, and in many ways, the child most like herself. Both Elizabeth and Thomas Peter were strong Baptists, yet they decided to have the ceremony on Edisto at Daniel's church. This was especially gratifying to Daniel, who had a special soft spot for his baby daughter. She was her daddy's darling. Reverend Lee, the Presbyterian pastor, was a family friend from the time Elizabeth was a little girl. Hephzibah wanted this final family wedding to be memorable, and Bella was determined that this wedding breakfast would outshine all the others, for Elizabeth was like her own child.

The mistress of Bleak Hall was nearing sixty now and feeling those years. Observing Daniel each day as he went about his activities made her keenly aware of how the years were weighing on him. He was close to eighty, and moving more slowly all the time. Daniel's mind, however, was sharp and clear, and his love of storytelling survived the years, much to the delight of his grandchildren who were growing in number every year.

Equally satisfying to Hephzibah was the growth of her beloved Baptist church. The year 1838 was a banner one because

Pastor William McDunn came as pastor for the congregation, and he was the classic opposite of his predecessor. Whereas Peter Ludlow was stiff and formal, uninvolved in the lives of his parishioners and constantly resentful of the status of Sister Townsend, Pastor McDunn was warm and caring, taking to heart the needs of all the people of his flock, irrespective of the color of their skin or the status they held. Here was a man after Hephzibah Townsend's own heart, and she daily thanked the good Lord for sending such a treasure to Edisto. Furthermore, McDunn and Daniel Townsend quickly became fast friends, and this was an added boon as far as his wife was concerned.

Hephzibah planned a special family celebration for Daniel's eightieth birthday in 1839. June 17 arrived, and all the children and their spouses were there for the big day. This was the most meaningful reception preparation Hephzibah and Bella had ever organized, for the family patriarch was somewhat of a legend on Edisto. One of the largest planters in the low country, Townsend was both admired and respected by the community as well as loved by his family.

For his part, Daniel decided to finish off his birthday by updating his will. It had remained unchanged for six years and in the meantime they had lost their Ben. Townsend also wanted to give Hephzibah more flexibility as to where she wished to live after he was gone. He made provision for her to have their town residence and felt that Shargould should be hers outright, for rather than Shargould going to Dr. Daniel, they assisted this son in purchasing the beautiful Fenwick Hall in 1840. This second son had lost two wives and been hard hit with grief. Henrietta

had died in childbirth — and the following year he married Mary
Walpole of John's Island, and then lost her to bilious fever. His
parents were grateful when Dr. Daniel met Susan Swinton and the
two of them married and settled down at Fenwick Hall on John's
Island. The plantation was fascinating to Hephzibah because of
its long and storied history, dating back to the first British owner
nearly 150 years earlier. Fenwick Hall itself was quite magnificent.

About this time, Edisto's Episcopal congregation was busy
with constructing a new building, and Hephzibah and Edisto
Baptist Church were able to help them out. Hephzibah possessed
lifelong friends among the membership of Trinity Episcopal. After
all, she had grown up often attending church there, where her
father had been a strong leader. Now Edisto Baptist welcomed the
Episcopal congregation to use their facilities during the building
process, so the Baptist sanctuary was used extensively for a period
of months. When the Episcopal congregation was able to move
into their new sanctuary, in order to honor Hephzibah Jenkins
Townsend a pew was set apart in their new building for her use
during her lifetime. Hephzibah was touched by the beautiful
gesture and smiled to think of how that would have gratified her
dear papa.

As Daniel grew increasingly frail, Hephzibah depended on
Bella to handle more and more of the catering and planning.
Bella's Lewis excelled in carpentry and now directed the workshop
on Bleak Hall Plantation, including training a number of young
servants in woodworking skills. Daniel began spending more
time indoors, resting and reading; he particularly loved having
the grandchildren come to visit. By 1842, he had ten of them and

doted on each one.

Both Hephzibah and Daniel were also spending more time in Charleston. One contributing factor was surely the grandchildren. Elizabeth's firstborn, the tiny Thomas, was born in April 1840 but died with a virulent fever in September. Elizabeth clung to her mother during her grief and gained strength from her encouraging presence. Sure enough, she had another baby the next year, and little Emma Julia Smith flourished. Elizabeth enjoyed teasing her mama, suggesting that she wanted to follow Hephzibah's example of being fruitful and multiplying.

The last year or so of Daniel Townsend's life was something like a golden twilight. He and Hephzibah formed the habit of sitting on the spacious front porch of Bleak Hall on pleasant evenings and reminiscing about days gone by. Sometimes they would reflect on those tragic times when their losses had been grievous, but more often their memories drifted to special moments that had brought joy. Hephzibah would tease Daniel about their courting days and how he had tried to wrap her in cotton wool, until he realized that, small and delicate as she appeared to be, looks were deceiving. A massive inner drive, that essential force of character, had been deeply embedded even in the young Hephzibah Jenkins. Tried in the crucible of tragedy and loss, it only strengthened over the years.

Hephzibah was wont to occasionally reflect on the times they violently disagreed, whether on a principle or on how to handle their land and property. Frequently Daniel would grin a bit ruefully and acknowledge that he had met his match. "Hephzibah," he commented one spring twilight, "I tried so hard to protect you. I wanted to be the one to provide for you, my dear," and Daniel paused and groped for words to express his heart, "but somehow you just did not need defending or protecting," and he reached over and grasped her hand. "Sometimes I felt like you simply didn't need me." His voice sounded a bit forlorn.

Hephzibah was quick to respond. "Never that, Daniel, just think back a moment. All right," and she paused to acknowledge, "I know I was raised to be independent and to have a mind of my own, but" — and she stopped and sought to find the words to explain what she meant — "sometimes it didn't matter how independent or capable I might be. I knew I was considered a mere woman," Hephzibah smiled a bit wryly over the words, "and those times, Daniel, when I couldn't meet the challenge without your help, you were always there for me." She thought a moment and added, "Husband, I don't recall telling you how much it meant to me when you personally gave a large gift to our society missions offering." She hesitated a moment. "You have never given me a gift I appreciated more." Tears welled in her eyes as she continued, "And you saved the church property for my dear people at Edisto Baptist." She paused. "Daniel, then you defended me so strongly when Pastor Ludlow would have undone the work of years," and she choked with emotion.

Daniel grasped her hand in a surprisingly strong grip. "But my very own dear, your sense of justice was on the firing line, and you know how that has always moved me mightily. I meant what I said that night I proposed to you, a whole lifetime ago." He stopped a moment and reflected, "I still see before me a beautiful person who possesses a quiet dignity and whose force of character drives that sense of justice." And now his own eyes filmed over, "Those traits of yours, my own Hephzibah, have only gotten stronger these many years." And Daniel hesitated before concluding, "Hephzibah, don't you know that your strength is my strength?" Hephzibah impulsively reached over and touched his face with the back of her hand. Daniel was so dear to her. He clasped her hand even more tightly, and the two sat in the shadows of the evening thinking back over the years they had lived together.

On a warm spring morning just weeks later, Hephzibah reached over as she always did to rouse Daniel to prepare for the day. This time the hand she touched was cold; God had taken him quietly and peacefully that morning of May 21, 1842. Daniel Townsend III had lived a rich and productive life for eighty-three years, but now part of Hephzibah's own heart was gone.

Word spread quickly and the family gathered, rallying around their mother. 'Rinthia was a special blessing to Hephzibah those difficult days, and when Hephzibah stood with her family gathered in the Jenkins family cemetery, the thoughts of nearly fifty years of saying goodbye to beloved beings in this place engulfed her mind in memories. She could only give thanks that Daniel died so peacefully, just going to sleep and waking in the presence of the Lord.

John Ferrars, as the oldest son, was looked to for family leadership, of course. He was, as always, most courteous to his mother, but now added to that was a special bit of tenderness which she had seldom noted in him. Sometimes it seemed with this son that she had to cross vast canyons of indifference to reach him. The two of them had not been particularly close, for they differed on several essential issues, but their love for each other was never in doubt. According to the will, Bleak Hall was to go to John, but he was careful not to sound presumptuous and sought his mother's wishes in how she wished to handle the transition. Hephzibah assured him that she wished to move quite soon, that she wanted to live at Shargould when she was at home on Edisto. Part of the time she would plan to stay in the town house in Charleston. "John," she sounded reassuring, "you know how special Shargould has always been to me. I always feel close to Brother when I am there, and that means a lot. I lost him far too early."

John offered all the assistance he could provide for his mother during the transition. A sore spot between them had long been the difference in the way they looked at slavery and all it meant in their lives as planters. Many of the servants would move with Hephzibah. She had grieved for years over John's stance, over his sense of entitlement, and in turn John had always felt that his mother was far too indulgent. As they made plans for her move, Hephzibah dared to bring up the subject of their difference of opinion once more. "Son," she spoke softly, "I have always appreciated the fact that you have treated me with real courtesy. You have never been offensive or negligent, but, John" — and she looked pleadingly into his keen blue eyes, so like his father's — "courtesy is fine, yet what I really want to see in you is compassion. When I am gone, please do not forget that," she concluded as she turned to walk to the next room, leaving those penetrating words hanging in the air.

— Twenty-Eight —

1842-1845
ENDING STRONG

It was like a piece of herself was missing. Never in Hephzibah's memory had she been without Daniel, and now there was this yawning emptiness without his presence. A hundred times a day she caught herself wanting to tell him something and ask his opinion; she tried to tire herself out during the full days so she could fall asleep at night of exhaustion. But try though she might, many a night Hephzibah could not keep from crying herself to sleep, praying for the mercy and comfort she found only in seeking it from her heavenly guide. Hephzibah Townsend had never before been so glad to be too busy. First, there was the move to Shargould, and of course her many responsibilities with the church and the missionary society. 'Rinthia was her mainstay, along with Bella, whose tender heart was quick to sense the needs of her cherished Miz Hephzibah, and she quietly went about helping in unobtrusive ways.

The more time Hephzibah spent in Charleston, the more she and Bella cut back on their business activities. Thankfully, the church was prospering and the society going strong, and a flock of grandchildren was a balm to her grieving soul.

Each clever word uttered by a grandchild made her eager to share it with Daniel, but now she couldn't. That was one of her hardest adjustments, this aching emptiness. Hephzibah wept tears that mingled with sorrow and joy when Elizabeth gave birth in August to a son, naming him Daniel Townsend. His grandmother prayed he would one day be a special tribute to his name and heritage. By the end of that first year without Daniel, Hephzibah had fourteen grandchildren and they were both her solace and her delight.

Whatever would she do without her Bella? Hephzibah had lost count of the people who wished they, too, had such help. Elizabeth and her Thomas frequently exchanged letters with Dr. and Mrs. Manly, now living in Alabama. The two families shared a lasting friendship. Hephzibah happened to be in Charleston when one of Manly's letters arrived, and Elizabeth laughed as she began to read, handing her mother the sheet of correspondence so she could see Basil Manly's request. He had written: "Tell your good old mother, I wish she would get in a liberal fit one of these days and send me Bella. I shall never get done thanking any body that will send me a servant who will be faithful and will take care of wife and the children when the good woman is sick." To which Hephzibah retorted, "Tell Dr. Manly this good old mother doesn't have liberal fits like that!"

Dr. Manly particularly enjoyed hearing reports of the progress of the Edisto church, for he felt a personal investment in it. Hephzibah knew her heart was there, for she had literally invested her energies and interests in the people who made up that congregation. One of her deepest satisfactions came from knowing that, at this church, people who were enslaved nonetheless held positions of leadership. This was not true with any other denomination on Edisto, nor was it true in other Baptist congregations in the low country. At Edisto Baptist, not only were all the members able to be part of attending to church business, but slaves also took leadership roles as deacons.

Here was a true sense of communal identity, and this touched and blessed everyone in the congregation. Associations of sisterhood and brotherhood were deeply rooted in the Gullah culture that had come with the slaves from West Africa, and these flourished at the church. Hephzibah especially loved the warmth and spirit of the music in the services. The rhythm was infectious, and Hephzibah would find her very heart swaying to the depth and richness in the music each Sunday. By contrast, the more staid and formal services in the Charleston church seemed sadly lacking after the spirit of worship found at Edisto Baptist. Hephzibah could not fail to recognize in those songs the members loved that hope and eternity and the freedom to be found in Christ were constant themes, and she could understand that. They must surely long for freedom. It also planted a salutary thorn in her conscience with each such refrain.

Even if it pricked her conscience, Hephzibah nonetheless loved the music and its spirit. Every service included the grand hymns of the faith and also songs that held particular import for the enslaved of the congregation. When they sang "Balm In Gilead" or "Nobody Knows the Trouble I Seen," and "Sweet Little Jesus Boy," it never failed to stir her heart. The voices raised in song here were pure worship. The effect was like wrapping yourself in a warm quilt, so personal and rich it was.

Hephzibah always tried to be on Edisto when it was the day

for the mite society to meet. The trials and tribulations, the joys and growth of the missions work in Burmah and China were matters of prayer and rejoicing for these women who felt part of the work ten thousand miles away. Late in 1844, they learned that young Henrietta Hall Shuck died in childbirth, leaving a sorrowing husband and four small children. Henrietta was only twenty-seven and not a few tears were shed over that grievous news.

'Rinthia and Hephzibah often commented on the blessing that was theirs on the Wadmalaw-Edisto Missionary Society. It was the only place in their lives where women had autonomy, able to make the decisions they felt God wanted for the group. It had been an uplifting experience and one of their great joys. By contrast, church polity was very much a man's world. 'Rinthia commented one afternoon on Hephzibah's talent for involving the men in her life in navigating those paths where a woman was not permitted to make decisions. "Sister," she grinned, "you have become an expert negotiator. And you know, Daniel might have gotten exasperated with you time and again, but," and 'Rinthia reached over and caught her sister's hand, "he loved you so much and he showed it time and again." And Hephzibah's tears spilled over as she recalled those many times when Daniel came to her rescue.

Pastor McDunn was another such supporter, caring deeply for his flock and reaping the benefits of Sister Townsend's many years of experience at the church. The two met to plan the Christmas revival that year of 1844, and Hephzibah proposed trying something new. "Pastor," she suggested, "since we always have these services around Christmas when the servants have time off in the evenings, let us meet this year at my home at Shargould."

Reverend McDunn's face lit up. "Sister Townsend, I think the congregation would be thrilled. It will make the services especially meaningful to them that way. But tell me," he paused to think it over, "do you think there is enough room there?" Hephzibah quickly assured him that by using the parlor at Shargould, which opened up into the dining area and the hallway beyond, they would be able to accommodate everyone. Then McDunn had another thought, "But there is the question of baptizing any new converts. You know we normally do that at the conclusion of our special meetings."

Hephzibah smiled broadly, "Pastor, I think there is a solution for that," and she asked, "Are you familiar with those new tin tubs?" McDunn looked a little puzzled. "Bella's son Lewis, you know him," Hephzibah reminded him. "Well, Lewis is a very clever carpenter. He has made me a large tub constructed of sheet copper. And he actually made a wooden box to set it in and you can move it around. Very clever!" She concluded, "How about the tub for our baptizing?" Her pastor was delighted and plans for the services proceeded apace.

Beginning December 21, the special meetings began and sure enough, Hephzibah's parlor and most of the ground floor were crowded with members and visitors coming for meeting time. 'Rinthia came on the evenings she could and Amarinthia came from Peter's Point to help Hephzibah host the services. The music was glorious, both the Christmas carols and the wonderful spirituals that lifted the soul. They began each evening around seven, when the servants were through with their daily tasks. For the entire week, they never ended before midnight. Hephzibah would fall into bed exhausted each night, but it was a happy exhaustion. By the final two nights, numbers came to faith and gave stirring testimonials of what God had done for them. Hephzibah was frequently close to tears, but never more so than when Lewis made a profession of faith. Bella was glowing.

On the final night, there was a real sense of community and excitement. The men who served as deacons assisted Pastor McDunn and Sister Townsend in baptizing the sixty converts in the new tub, and from Abraham to Diana and Juliet to Wally, the new believers testified to their faith and were immersed. Services the final night went on past midnight and left memories never to be forgotten. William McDunn could look back on no other time in his many years of ministry that gave him greater joy, and Hephzibah felt that her small reach for meaning was gloriously realized that week of revival. Edisto Baptist Church now had a membership exceeding 450.

A week later, the year 1845 arrived and life seemed to get back to a more normal routine. Hephzibah had been dealing with an idea for many months now and decided it was time to talk it over with Bella. Those two had a unique bond. Maybe they were mistress and servant, but that did not adequately explain their relationship. Bella was an integral part of Hephzibah Townsend's life, and now Hephzibah reached a decision. One January night after the usual busyness of the day, Hephzibah asked Bella to come to her study for a talk.

They began with talking over the wonderful happenings

of the revival services and then Hephzibah got to the point. "Bella," she began, "I have been considering something for a long time now. I want to talk it over with you." Hephzibah hesitated, finding it difficult to put her thoughts into words. It had been on her heart for years now, steadily growing into a conviction. It was something she must do. It was something she wanted to do. "Surely you must know what you have meant to me these many years," and Hephzibah choked up a bit. Bella was looking anxious and wondering if Miz Hephzibah was feeling bad or had a big problem. "You have been with me, dear friend and helper, since the day you came into this world. And Bella, you have blessed my world," and Hephzibah paused to control her emotions.

"The Mite Society and our church, these would never have happened, Bella, without you," and she reached out and gently touched the side of Bella's face. "You have made the difference." Bella broke in exclaiming, "Oh, Miz Hephzibah, this is my calling. These are the things God put me on this earth to do. I know that."

"Bella," Hephzibah responded, "I know that there is a tide in the affairs of men, and I hope I have not missed mine." Bella looked puzzled and Hephzibah continued, "I know very well what the law says. I also know that the law says you cannot teach slaves to read and write. However," she stopped and smiled, "we managed to do that anyway here at Bleak Hall, didn't we, just like Papa did when I was growing up."

Bella gave a broad smile, "Thank God for that, Miz Hephzibah, my being able to read and write opened up so much of this world to me. I am thankful for that." Hephzibah smiled at this expression of gratitude on the part of the younger woman,

"Dear Bella, you recall you've heard me say time and again what Papa taught me long ago: 'To him that wills, ways are not wanting.' Well," she added, "I would reshape the law if I could. Maybe we can find a way around it."

"What are you talking about, Miz Hephzibah? I'm not real sure the point of this," and Bella's face reflected her bewilderment. Hephzibah reached out and grasped Bella's hand. Looking down at her wrinkled white hand holding the smooth and capable brown one, she explained, "You and I, Bella, we have a special bond. And Bella," Hephzibah found it difficult to continue, "I wish to give you your freedom. You have more than earned it."

Now the brown hand compulsively clutched the white one and tears rolled down Bella's cheeks, "Miz Hephzibah, my heart is free. It always has been. You've seen to that. But just think a minute. What would I do with my freedom now? Where would I go? My life is here, my mission is here." Hephzibah began to look distraught, but Bella quickly assured her, "Oh no, oh no, I'm not resentful. I mean it. But," and here she took a deep breath, "I would like to offer another idea."

"Of course, of course, Bella, what do you have in mind?" Hephzibah questioned. Bella softly smiled and suggested, "Miz Hephzibah, how about me accepting that offer of freedom — for my own Lewis? I would love to see my son be free; that would thrill this mother's heart of mine!" In that moment the two women — one old, one not so old — sat in perfect unity of heart and wept together. And then being the two women they were, they quickly set to work planning how Lewis could set himself up in the construction business in Charleston. Freedom. It would be like a dream come true. All of Lewis's years of faithful work and training would stand him in good stead now.

And before the two friends said goodnight, they spent some moments in prayer together, asking God to open the way and give them wisdom. Hephzibah went to bed that evening more contented than she had been in many a long month. Sorrows had been frequent and tragedies had abounded, but the multiplied blessings of God far outweighed the grief. That winter night, the mother of many and grandmother of even more, the framer of a missions society and founder of a church fell asleep with a sense of quiet and peace she had not felt in years. And Bella joyfully hurried in the direction of Lewis's cottage to tell him the stunning news. God was making a way.

Grave of Hephzibah Jenkins Townsend, 1780-1847, located at Edisto Island Baptist Church.

Epilogue

Hephzibah Jenkins Townsend died March 4, 1847, some two months prior to her sixty-seventh birthday. History records only that the cause of death was a sudden illness. Exactly what illness is not known. Nonetheless, Hephzibah had earlier been very clear about her wishes when she died. It was her request that she be buried in the cemetery of her beloved Baptist church. This was highly unusual, since her husband had been interred at the Presbyterian church. She had determined, even in death, to align herself with her chosen denomination. Hephzibah's children honored her request. To this day, she is the lone white person buried at Edisto Baptist Church, and she continues to be revered by that congregation.

The inscription on her monument reads:

> Her character was so strongly cast, and her impulses were so generous that she was an object of indifference to no one. The poor and the afflicted were special objects of her consideration. By these her loss is truly felt. And by us who knew her best is she most lamented. From early life she professed the gospel of Jesus Christ and her faith continued firm and steadfast to the end. With this, she blended so much humility that her most frequent religious confession was, "I am a sinner saved by grace." She rests amid

the scenes of her piety and her bounty, a pattern
of Christian trial and Christian faith.

Hephzibah's obituary drew attention to her constant affirmation that her God was her Polar Star. It went on to state
instances of her liberality and graciousness, also saying:

Frailties, indeed she had, for frailty is incident to
human nature, but hers were the honest perver-
sions of an honorable mind and flowed naturally
from her virtues. Her good deeds will long be
remembered, whilst her faults have almost been
swallowed upon the grave and to us ... will her
memory long be sacred as of one of the good
who has passed away.

And somewhat astoundingly, the fruits of her remarkable
life continue to make a difference, as women across the country,
and, indeed around the world, follow in her footsteps in caring for
others and sharing the good news of Jesus Christ through groups
just such as the one she first organized.

Those six of Hephzibah's fifteen children who lived to
adulthood lived to honor her name and to live fruitful, productive
lives. Only Susan Martha never married. She lived with her sister
Elizabeth in Charleston and was the children's beloved "Aunt
Sunie," continuing her life of service through her church and
missionary society. Mary Frampton Pope became the mother of
five. Amarinthia Jenkins Mikell had seven children, John Ferrars

and his wife, four. Dr. Daniel Jenkins Townsend and his last wife also had four children — and the youngest daughter, Elizabeth Townsend Smith, outdid them all, giving birth to twelve, eight of whom lived to adulthood. Hephzibah and Daniel's great-grandchildren were legion in number, and there are countless descendants to this day. Many of them became well-known leaders in their cities and states.

The Townsend offspring lived privileged and productive lives, although the effects of the war that tore the nation apart were quite devastating. Mary Frampton Pope was one of the founding leaders of the Brick Baptist Church on St. Helena. She and John built a lovely home on their St. Helena Sea Island Cotton plantation in the 1850s and named it The Oaks. Union troops occupied the mansion during the war, and it became the first school for freedmen in the United States. Thomas Peter Smith and Elizabeth lived in a lovely home in Charleston, and Dr. Daniel Jenkins Townsend and his wife, Susan, resided in the mansion called Fenwick Hall on John's Island. It was a showplace. Amarinthia Jenkins Townsend and her Isaac Jenkins Mikell lived at Peter's Point on Edisto, and Isaac began building their elegant Charleston town house in 1851. Amarinthia died in 1852 before she could enjoy it, although it was basically the fortune she brought to the marriage that made the house possible. Of course, John Ferrars Townsend and his wife, Caroline, lived at Bleak Hall.

Two of Hephzibah Jenkins Townsend's quilts are preserved in the Smithsonian Institute and can be viewed online. One quilt is the early Hawk and Owl motif, and the other is the Tree of Life, exhibiting beautiful birds, butterflies and flowers. It is a child's quilt.

The church established by Hephzibah Townsend in 1818 is flourishing today and carrying on the traditions begun there nearly two hundred years ago. The sunken baptistery to the side of the church has been filled in for safety reasons, but its outline is easy to see. Every year when the Edisto Historical Society holds its tour of homes, Edisto Baptist is on the circuit and traditionally has all-day singing and dinner on the grounds (although most eat inside in the fellowship hall!). Listening to the soul-stirring music in the auditorium is a trip back in time. One can almost turn around and see a smiling Hephzibah sitting on one of the pews, keeping time to the music. The church is justly proud of its heritage and loves to entertain visitors. Edisto Baptist Church has been lovingly restored. There is a new structure sitting next to it, but the original building is still maintained and used upon occasion. One can see the original bell, the strong hardwood floors and tabby foundation built to last. The remains of Hephzibah's and Bella's tabby ovens also can be seen standing near the water's edge at Frampton's Inlet. Both places are on the National Register of Historic Places and have an aura of timelessness about them.

One of the great legacies of Hephzibah Jenkins Townsend was the respect and dignity afforded the slave membership during those early years. In this place like no other, a man and a woman had voices and opinions that mattered and were free to exercise their leadership skills. The church provided for them an answer to two longings of their hearts, longings for meaning and community. It was a gift on which no price could be placed. Their lives mattered, and they found in the church the shelter of communal identity. Lending them a sense of dignity was very important to Sister

Townsend, and perhaps this was one of the legacies afforded her by her beloved Maum Jean. Just how long she lived after saving Hephzibah's life is not known, but clearly her influence was profound.

Hephzibah Jenkins Townsend was far ahead of her time. She learned how to work within the framework of her society. If it had to be a man to make a certain decision, she learned how to bring that about in order to achieve her goals. Certainly Hephzibah and Daniel had frequent "domestic difficulties," but all the available letters, records and stories make clear the bond of love and loyalty that never deserted them. Daniel might have vehemently disagreed with something Hephzibah did or said, but he unfailingly supported and protected her.

Hephzibah Townsend met her moment, and her legacy blessed not only her family and countless descendants but continues to bear fruit today around the world through the organization known as Woman's Missionary Union. It all began with a small group of women meeting at Bleak Hall in 1811, enjoying fresh gingerbread and enlarging their borders to embrace the world.

Author's Note

When researching the history of national Woman's Missionary Union, the figure of the founder of the first missionary society in the South jumped off the pages. Hephzibah Jenkins Townsend fascinated me. Thus began three years of research into her life and legacy, along with a number of trips to Edisto Island and Charleston, South Carolina, walking the paths where she walked two hundred years ago. In shaping her life's story, I took all available materials from archives and records, piecing together what formed this incredible woman who was so far ahead of her time. She stretched the boundaries of her day and has left an indelible memory and legacy.

Hephzibah was a figure of her time in history that could not be ignored. In light of the paucity of letters and documents — so many of which were destroyed in the fire that swept Bleak Hall, in addition to all those lost during the War between the States — I developed her personality and voice based on available materials. The voice I gave her perforce had to somewhat become my own, as I looked at her actions and achievements and formed them into the whole of what she accomplished.

So little was written about opinions concerning slavery in that period when it was such an accepted way of life. The evidence of Hephzibah Townsend's life and work give certainty to the fact that she was different. I found repeatedly in stories and documents related to her life that she constantly affirmed, "These are my people," in referring to those who were enslaved. She did not, however, do that in a patronizing way. It was a genuine expression of her inward conviction. Not one time did she forget the debt she owed Maum Jean and Jack, who had literally saved her life. Records do not reveal how long the old couple lived, but it is very clear that Maum Jean had a lasting influence on Hephzibah Jenkins Townsend, whose life she had saved at the risk of her own.

The archives at Furman University contain some fascinating material related to Edisto Baptist Church. The book of minutes recorded by Rev. William McDunn between 1838 and 1845 is a treasure trove and is reflective of his gracious spirit and loving heart. Pastor McDunn listed by name the sixty slaves who were baptized at the end of the December revival. By contrast, the vitriol in the scathing four-page letter Rev. Peter Ludlow sent Hephzibah Townsend in 1832 is shocking. The pages are scorched with animus.

I have made a consistent effort to remain true to the broad historical background, hence the repeated trips and continuing research. One of the great joys has been getting to know, either in person or by phone, several of Hephzibah's descendants, and they are an impressive group. What a heritage they have! In turn, I can look at their meaningful lives and know that she would have been justly proud of them.

I took occasional liberties with time. It is evident that Hephzibah's plan was to free Bella, but she died quite suddenly before that took place. Bella was then offered her freedom by Susan Martha and she instead accepted it for her son Lewis. Lewis became a prosperous businessman in Charleston, constructing homes and using the talents he had honed as a child at Bleak Hall.

Bella must have found great joy in his freedom. The laws of South Carolina at that time made it extremely difficult to free a slave, but the Townsends managed anyway. Census records of the 1800s show that there were several free black people living at Bleak Hall Plantation. Their stories, were they known, would surely make interesting tales to read.

It is likely that the beautiful little icehouse, shaped like a chapel and still standing, was built during the time of John Ferrars Townsend, although the records are not clear.

A few of the diseases and illnesses that claimed the lives of Hephzibah's children were recorded. Others are lost to history, so the biography alludes to the most prominent of the illnesses that ended in death during those particular years. Bilious fever — which caused severe vomiting — was often mentioned, and malaria affected many, as did yellow fever and dysentery.

A number of historical figures appear in Hephzibah's story. Richard Furman and the Furman family were very much a part of the Townsends' circle of friends and acquaintances, and Hephzibah Townsend revered her pastor and depended on him. Her friendship with Rachel is likely; however, the friendship of Rachel's sisters and Hephzibah's two oldest daughters are based on records of extensive correspondence between the Furman and Townsend girls in the 1820s. These are on file in the archives of the James B. Duke Library at Furman University. Likewise, the friendship of the Basil Manlys and the Townsends is based on actual documents, as is the friendship of the Manlys with Elizabeth Townsend and Thomas Peter Smith in Charleston. Many letters survive that the families wrote to one another.

Captain Daniel Jenkins and Charles Cotesworth Pinckney were contemporaries and both served in government. Hephzibah and Pinckney's daughter Eliza were born the same year, and their homes in Charleston were less than two blocks apart. The Jenkinses' children and the Townsends' offspring all had tutors and governesses, but their names are not known.

The Grimkes of Charleston were acquaintances of the Townsends, and Thomas Grimke was the Townsends' lawyer. Grimke's two sisters, Sarah and Angelina, were well-known figures in that period and were quite notorious in Charleston because of their abolitionist views. It is highly likely that they were an influence on Hephzibah. Hephzibah's views on slavery are based on the preponderance of evidence found in her actions, especially her close relationship with Bella and her founding of the church, primarily for "her people." Views on slavery attributed to Furman and Manly are also based on historical record.

The story of the miraculous escape of the infant Hephzibah from Charleston is pieced together from an abundance of existing documents and tales written of the experience. There is no complete record of which relative cared for little Daniel Jr. and kept the baby until Captain Daniel Jenkins was released from prison, but the bulk of evidence and the close proximity of Abigail Jenkins Murray's home to the Jenkins plantation makes her the likely candidate. She and Captain Daniel were double first cousins and friends as well.

It was fascinating to discover that the family had a portrait made of Maum Bella. Unfortunately, there is no known portrait of Hephzibah Jenkins Townsend. There are however, several descriptions of her as small, with delicate features, shiny black hair and deep-set dark eyes. Her personality traits were also repeatedly recorded. It would be hard to overlook those frequent descriptions of her "quiet dignity, force of character, and sense of justice." She was a force in her day, and her memory lingers on like the fragrance of those Carolina jessamine clustered around the porch of the house on Calhoun Street.

ACKNOWLEDGEMENTS

A number of people have helped search out the remarkable woman who founded the missionary society movement among Baptist women in the South. In the forefront have been Laurie Register, executive director-treasurer of South Carolina WMU, and the inspiring women who make up that organization in Hephzibah Jenkins Townsend's home state.

The members of Edisto Baptist Church, Edisto Island, South Carolina, founded by Hephzibah in 1818, do her name proud as they serve faithfully in this millennium. They were an inspiration, with their love for their history and appreciation for those who have gone before. Deborah Robinson of New York, and a descendant of early members of the church, was a special encouragement as I did research.

Much appreciation is due the fine staff of Edisto Museum, who are exceptionally knowledgeable about the Bleak Hall treasures in their collection.

Many thanks also go to the archivists at the James B. Duke Library of Furman University, Addlestone Library of the College of Charleston, the South Caroliniana Library of the University of South Carolina, and the South Carolina Historical Society in Charleston. Cindy Johnson, archivist of National Woman's Missionary Union, provided excellent assistance with early WMU history.

A debt of gratitude goes to historian Carol Hardy Bryan of Edgefield, South Carolina, for her invaluable assistance in research in the Duke Library. It was a labor of love on her part to delve into files about the remarkable Hephzibah Townsend. She approached it as if she was working on her own family's genealogy, and surely it is a record of our family of Baptist women. Thanks also go to Jane Poster, archivist for the South Carolina Baptist Convention, for valuable help in research and to David George, president of WMU Foundation, SBC, for consistent encouragement and support. Another source of affirmation and information was WMU leader Lil Drawdy of Hampton, South Carolina.

A special bonus has been the assistance of direct lineal descendants of Hephzibah Jenkins Townsend herself, especially historian Dr. Charles Spencer of Arlington, Virginia, and archivist Mrs. Alicia (Lish) Thompson of Charleston, South Carolina. They do honor to their ever-so-great-grandmother. Mr. Jack Boineau of Adams Run, South Carolina, was a great source of help and inspiration the last two years of his life. Mr. and Mrs. Boineau lived in The Summit, the house built by Hephzibah's beloved sister Amarinthia.

Hephzibah would not have been able to tell her story had it not been for two gifted editors, Iva Jewel Tucker and Ella Robinson, both of Birmingham, Alabama. They are peerless.

Hephzibah Jenkins Townsend has left a legacy to each of us in this generation. May we, as she, pass on to those who follow our own legacies of devotion to God's service.

Sources

Baker, Robert S. and Paul J. Craven. *Adventures in Faith: The First 300 Years of First Baptist Church, Charleston, South Carolina.* Nashville, Tennessee: Broadman Press, 1882.

Bolls, Kate McChesney. *The Daniel Townsends of the South Carolina Islands.* Verona, Virginia: McClure Printing Co., Inc., 1975.

Charleston Courier. 1803-1846.

College of Charleston, Charleston, South Carolina. Archives — Hephzibah Jenkins Townsend Files, Addlestone Library.

Edisto Island Baptist Church papers. Baptist Historical Collection, James B. Duke Library, Furman University, Greenville, South Carolina.

Furman, Rev. Richard and Family, Papers. Baptist Historical Collection, James B. Duke Library, Furman University, Greenville, South Carolina.

Hephzibah Jenkins Townsend and Thomas Peter Smith files. James B. Duke Library, Furman University, Greenville, South Carolina.

Graydon, Nell S. *Tales of Edisto.* Orangeburg: Sandlapper Publishing Co., Inc. 1955.

Hamilton, Virginia. *The People Could Fly: American Black Folktales.* Knopf: New York, 1985.

Manly, Basil Sr. "*From the Diary of Basil Manly, Sr.,*" 19 July 1922, *Baptist Courier.*

McIntosh, Sherrie L. *The Old Edisto Island Baptist Church.*

Hephzibah Jenkins Townsend: 1780-1847 and the Inheritance of Stewardship and Spiritual Gifts. Morgantown, West Virginia. University of West Virginia, 1998.

Minutes of the General Committee of the Charleston Baptist Association, 1812, 5. Baptist Historical Collection, Furman University, Greenville, South Carolina.

Puckette, Clara Childs. *Edisto: A Sea Island Principality.* Cleveland: Seaforth Publications, 1978.

Townsend, John: Family Papers. Caroliniana Library, University of South Carolina, Columbia, South Carolina.

Spencer, Charles. *Edisto Island 1663-1860: Wild Eden to Cotton Aristocracy.* The History Press, 2008.

Spencer, Charles. *The Murray Family Of Edisto Island South Carolina.* Arlington, Virginia, 2011.

Spencer, Charles. *Documents on Edisto Island History.* Edisto Island, South Carolina, The Edisto Island Historic Preservation Society.

Webber, Deborah G. "Descendants of John Jenkins of St. Johns Colleton." *The South Carolina and Genealogical Magazine.* 20 October 1919.

Will of Daniel Jenkins, 6 June 1804, Book A, 1800-1807, page 109. Record of Wills, Charleston County, South Carolina.

CPSIA information can be obtained
at www.ICGtesting.com
Printed in the USA
FFOW04n1818080717
37465FF